AGCIM

Namasté!

Charlotte McGinn

What people are saying about
A Golf Course in Miracles:

"Gene Bogart has the same kind of wild sense of humor that I do… Charlotte McGinnis is obviously a kindred spirit. That sense of humor is readily apparent in this fun, clever and profound book, *A Golf Course in Miracles.*

"If you play golf, your game will never be the same, only better. And if you're reading this book for the humor and the wisdom, you won't be disappointed. You would have to know the Course very well to write this book.

"If, like me, you love the Course, it will be easy for you to love this book. And even if you're not a student of *A Course in Miracles,* you'll find much to learn as well as much to smile at in these pages. It may not help you get a hole in one, but it will help you realize we *all are* one…

"Thanks, Gene and Charlotte, for the cool book, and for reminding us that *A Course in Miracles* is a happy form of spirituality!"

—from the *Foreword* written by **Gary Renard**, bestselling author of *The Disappearance of the Universe* and *Your Immortal Reality*

"It's often said that we are spiritual beings having a physical experience. If so, then it makes perfect sense that everyday life holds the key to powerful spiritual lessons—including life on the golf course! In *A Golf Course in Miracles*, golf-pro and the former Executive Director of the *Palm Beach Center for Living*, Charlotte McGinnis, and co-author Gene Bogart, masterfully remind us that powerful lessons await in the seemingly insignificant moments of life—whether we're on the golf course, in the classroom, or in our living room. The key to unleashing their power hinges upon our ability, and willingness, to recognize them.

"With laser-like precision and a down-to-earth style this book is about you, me, our world and the rich lessons found in everyday experience. Whether you're an athlete, artist or an engineer, this book is about you, your world, and every relationship that you'll ever experience in life."

— *Gregg Braden*, New York Times bestselling author of *The Divine Matrix*, and *Fractal Time*

"Charlotte and Gene have delivered a wonderful gift to all who desire to have the rich teachings of the Course shared in a voice that is clear, funny, and highly insightful. These insights illuminated for me the deeper meanings of the Course and how to practically integrate them into our lives.

"As a golfer, I absolutely loved the metaphors, as I have always thought that golf is a truly spiritual game. This gem of a book reveals truths that will make the pursuit of personal mastery far easier than mastering the game of golf!"

— *Marcus Gillette*, acclaimed author and presenter *(with wife Sheila)* of *The Teachings of THEO*

" *'You are not your golf score,'* is a well-known quote, but a very hard one for golfers to accept. Ego puts up a tough fight.

"But in *A Golf Course in Miracles,* McGinnis and Bogart demonstrate over and over again the fallacy of tying your enjoyment of the game totally to a number. Their concept of a universal force as a *She* makes total sense when considering that the message is about love, and the female image is a better fit.

"If you wish to take the tension out of your game, *'Miracles'* gives you the game plan!"

— **Gary Wiren, Ph.D.** – Pro Golfer, Teacher, Author, TV Host – Member: PGA Hall of Fame

"Something tells me that *A Golf Course in Miracles* isn't really about improving your golf game, because I don't play golf, and I'm getting a tremendous amount of value from each lesson. The 'life is a game of golf' metaphor is fun to play with and keeps each lesson fresh and engaging. Makes me want to start playing golf so I can learn more about how to play full out in life!"

— **Dr. W. Bradford Swift**, Founder & Chief Visionary Officer, Life On Purpose Institute; author of *Life On Purpose: Six Passages to an Inspired Life*

A
Golf Course
in
Miracles

BY
CHARLOTTE MCGINNIS
AND GENE BOGART

FOUNDATION FOR INNER PAR

A Golf Course in Miracles

ISBN: 0983396302
ISBN-13: 978-0-9833963-0-7

Published by the Foundation for Inner Par

For information, contact: *http://www.AGCIM.com*
Email: *info@agcim.com*

(Details on contacting the authors can be found in the
Notes & Links section in the back of this book.)

Table of Contents:

ACKNOWLEDGEMENTS   1
FOREWORD (BY GARY RENARD)   5
INTRODUCTION (BY GENE BOGART)   9
PRELUDE (BY CHARLOTTE MCGINNIS)   13

THE FRONT NINE

Hole 1: I need par nothing.   19
Hole 2: My drive holds only what I swing with God.   25
Hole 3: No fairway I see means anything.   31
Hole 4: I do not know what any club is for.   37
Hole 5: I tee nothing as it is now.   43
Hole 6: I am upset because I slice a ball that is not there. 49
Hole 7: I see only the past (in this sand trap.)   55
Hole 8: My mind is preoccupied with past strokes.   61
Hole 9: My putts do not mean anything.   67

THE BACK NINE

Hole 10: God is in every green I see.   73
Hole 11: God is in every green I see because God is in
          my golf bag.   77
Hole 12: I am not the victim of the hole I bogey.   81
Hole 13: There is another way of looking at this wood.   87
Hole 14: God plays with me wherever I go.   95
Hole 15: My hooks are images I have made.   99
Hole 16: I have no neutral stance; I see no neutral grip. 107
Hole 17: I seek but what score belongs to me in truth.   115
Hole 18: God's Will for me is perfect follow through.   121

THE THIRD NINE

Hole 19: I am determined to birdie.   127
Hole 20: Above all else I want to eagle.   133
Hole 21: I can escape from the bunker I see by giving up
       hazard thoughts.   139
Hole 22: I do not perceive my own best handicap.   145
Hole 23: I have invented the rough I see.   153
Hole 24: There is no green my mashie niblick cannot reach.   159
Hole 25: Let me not forget my divot.   165
Hole 26: God is the caddie with which I play.   173
Hole 27: I am entitled to mulligans.   179

THE REAL 19TH HOLE
(A.K.A. "THE FINAL SCORE")

28: I could see the clubhouse instead of this.   187

ABOUT THE AUTHORS   193
NOTES & LINKS   197

Acknowledgments

• FROM CHARLOTTE •

First and foremost, I want to thank my wonderful parents for all of the opportunities, encouragement and support they have given to me. I appreciate you both more every day.

My sisters, Suzanne and Mollie, and my brother Kit, for not only being great siblings, but also wonderful friends.

To Arnold Browning, my first golf instructor and inspiration… I am so grateful to you for not only teaching me how to play the game, but also helping me to fall in love with it!

There have been so many mentors and teachers in my golf career who have given selflessly to me; I do my best every day to pay it forward. Thank you Paul Bailey, Robert Harper, Mike Krak, Mike Reynolds, Gary Wiren, George Lewis and Rick Vershure. There are so many more of you who taught me so much along the way – thank you so much!

I am so grateful to my spiritual teachers who have led and guided me on my journey, which has gotten me to the point where I am today. There have been many, and to all of you, I appreciate you and I thank you.

My partners in my businesses are a fabulous reflection in showing me that I have done something wonderful to have manifested such amazing people to share my vision with. Lindsay Babich, my partner in *Crowning Light Productions*, Lori Garcia-Hernandez, Karen King and Jennifer Byrd, my partners in *Fitness for the Body, Mind*

1

& *Soul*, and all of the talented hosts on the *Art of Living Well Radio Network*, Linda Marie Nelson, Nancy Ash, Margaret Ann Lembo, Gene Bogart and Lindsay Babich.

This book was an inspiration from my longtime friend and co-author, Gene Bogart. Without your divine idea a few years ago, *A Golf Course in Miracles* would have never happened. Thank you Gene, for your wisdom, wit and friendship.

I have been blessed in this life with my best friend and partner, Ellen Sherman. Ellen is truly an angel and lives by the messages conveyed in *AGCIM*. And also, Tootsie and Lola, my precious little dachshunds, continue to be an example of unconditional love and forgiveness…they are amazing teachers!

Acknowledgments

• FROM GENE •

To thank everyone who has been part of my growth over the last several decades in the areas of spirituality, metaphysics, and *A Course in Miracles* would require an entire book of its own, so please suffice it to say that I love you all, and my gratitude to you is endless. I do wish to personally recognize all of the members of the international study group that I am privileged to present, *On Course with Gene Bogart.* Your support and encouragement, every day, has been instrumental in allowing for the creation of this book, as well as our ongoing work together in our study of the Course itself. *Thank you, dear friends!*

Working as closely as I do with my buddy Gary Renard is both a privilege – and a blast! Listeners to our *Gary Renard Podcasts* tell us that it sounds like we're having a lot of fun doing these shows... and I assure you, we are! Gary, buddy, working with you in the studios as well as at so many live events has provided me with more opportunities than I would ever have imagined. For that *(and for writing our **Fore**-word!)*, you have my eternal gratitude...as well as simply for being one of my closest and most beloved friends.

My co-author, Charlotte McGinnis, is really like a family member; it was she, after all, who performed the wedding ceremony for Helen and I in 1998! Charlotte is also the person who, in any significant way, introduced me to the teachings of the Course itself. When the idea for the title *A Golf Course in Miracles* first popped into my head *(undoubtedly the work of the Holy Spirit!)*, there was not a moment's hesitation before I knew this was a project for Charlotte and I to work on together. Thank you, Char, for your love, professionalism,

3

encouragement *(and motivation)*, and for the joy and honor of collaborating with you on this book!

Our thanks to (and thanks *for*) our two adorable "nearly twin" sister tuxedo-kittens, Boots and Willie (just one year old as of the time of this writing.) Your appearance in our lives one year ago was assuredly the work of Spirit *(with perhaps some prodding from their late, big sister, Turbo)*. Thanks to all our "little girls" for their love, nuzzles, playing, and purring – and for always being our ongoing *furry forgiveness opportunities!*

And first and foremost, my lovely, talented, and beautiful wife, Helen, who has shared with me a level of unconditional love and support the likes of which I have never known before. Our coming together over fifteen years ago (in the hallway of the building that housed the *Palm Beach Center for Living*, no less!) was in no way an accident; it was the Holy Spirit's answer to my prayers, and the first of so many blessings that have followed. You have made my life as much like Heaven as anything on Earth can ever be, and without your endless support and tireless encouragement, this book *(along with so many other things)* would never have come into existence. I love you more than words could ever express…and you are, as always, *my Angel!*

Gene Bogart
South Florida
Summer, 2011

Foreword

*by **Gary Renard***

I first got to know Gene Bogart in the spring of 2003 after my first book *The Disappearance of the Universe* was published. A guy named Nelson had started an online discussion group at Yahoo about the book. Gene, who had joined, noticed along with me some of the things that were being said, and we realized we had a lot in common. We both had graduated from high school the same year, we were both the same age, and we had lived remarkably parallel lives. We both became professional guitar players and remained so for twenty years. While I was playing nightclubs and functions in New England, Gene, who was from Long Island, was doing the same, and also playing a glamour gig back and forth from New York to England on the ocean liner *Queen Elizabeth 2*. Nice work if you can get it. On top of that, we had both gotten into *A Course in Miracles*, and Gene appreciated my book. So did I; still being amazed that it had even been published, much less the fact that people were reading it.

About three years ago, Gene advised me that I should do a podcast. Being the high-tech person that I am, my response was, "A podcast. What's *that?*" Sensing my ineptitude, Gene offered to do the podcast with me as my on-air partner as well as the producer. Today, more than 43 podcasts later, Gene's brainchild has reached all over the world and helped introduce me to the many countries where the twenty translations of my books are available. And, as you listen, something else about Gene will strike you; he has the same kind of wild sense of humor that I do.

5

That sense of humor is readily apparent in this fun, clever and pro-found book, *A Golf Course in Miracles.* I don't personally know Gene's writing partner, Charlotte McGinnis, but I know her from these pages, and she's obviously a kindred spirit. If you play golf, your game will never be the same, only better. And if you're reading this book for the humor and the wisdom, you won't be disappointed. You would have to know the Course very well to write this book. You don't have to know the Course really well to enjoy it, but the better you know the Course the more fun it may be.

There are numerous take-offs on the Course here. For example, "Above all else I want to see," becomes, "Above all else I want to eagle." The book becomes a brilliant parody of the Workbook of *A Course in Miracles,* using golf as a metaphor for life, and its golf lessons as a metaphor for the Course. I appreciate the work and discipline that went into this book. Among other things, Gene facilitates his own on-line study group called *On Course.* There, he presents a lesson (and audio recording) from the Workbook of the Course every day, never missing a beat. A perfectionist, I've seen Gene work way beyond the call of duty to get every sound as clear as possible, every word as it should be. That dedication shows up as the written word in this book, and you the reader will benefit from Gene's determination to get things right.

Gene and his wife, Helen, and my wife Cindy and I have become four close friends. Whenever I host a Cruise for my readers to a lo-cation half way around the world, Gene and Helen are there to act as co-hosts and fellow entertainers. I may teach the Course for many hours, but when the evening comes or when we go on shore for an excursion, you can count on Gene and Helen to help Cindy and I join with all who are present, and make the many into one. That ability of Gene's, and also Charlotte's, is there to see throughout *A Golf Course in Miracles.*

If, like me, you love the Course, it will be easy for you to love this book. And even if you're not a student of *A Course in Miracles,*

6

you'll find much to learn as well as much to smile at in these pages. It may not help you get a hole in one, but it will help you realize we all are one, and that remembering to laugh is the first step in lightening up. And once you lighten up, can enlightenment be far behind?

Thanks, Gene and Charlotte, for the cool book, and for reminding us that *A Course in Miracles* is a happy form of spirituality. I've seen plenty of golfers out there suffering, but perhaps their time has come to be released, and all of us along with them.

Introduction

by Gene Bogart

The concept for this book came about several years before the book itself. I had been looking at the website of my dear friend (and now co-author) Charlotte McGinnis, and had noticed the title of something she had listed at her site: *"Zen Golf!"* What a great idea, I thought – combining Charlotte's proficiency as a golf instructor with her abundant knowledge of metaphysics!

And lo, the spark of an idea began to take shape…

I first met Charlotte almost twenty years ago (as of this writing), and it was she who, in any significant way, introduced me to the teachings of the magnificent thought system known as *A Course in Miracles*. Charlotte was, at that time, the founder and director of a wonderful volunteer outreach organization in South Florida known as *The Palm Beach Center for Living*. I became a 'regular volunteer' at the Center, whose activities and principles were based on the teachings of *A Course in Miracles* (also referred to as *"The Course,"* or simply, ACIM.) – *and don't worry; we'll be discussing a few of those memorable Center activities later in this book!*

Charlotte's experiences with *A Course in Miracles*, both as a student and as a teacher, go back well over twenty-five years. Her experience as a golf professional goes back even further; for over thirty years, she has been involved in professional competitive play, as well as being a sought-after "teaching pro" at a number of respected country clubs and golf organizations. So when I saw that *Zen Golf* reference at her website, the strange part of my mental landscape that's always coming up with odd and funny juxtapositions for things (I call that

9

part of my mind, *"the land where puns are born"*) instantly delivered to me the phrase that would become the title of the book that Charlotte and I would eventually write together: ***A Golf Course in Miracles!***

As you will see, various teachings and lesson titles from *A Course in Miracles* (ACIM) began to almost automatically 'morph' and transform their word structure to reflect, in often quite humorous ways, the combinations of *Golf* and *Course* conceptual material into what would become the chapter titles for *A Golf Course in Miracles* (AGCIM). We initially envisioned the book as having eighteen chapters, which seemed to be a quite inspired number, considering our golf theme – but then a greater number of irresistible titles continued to present themselves, until we had a total of twenty-seven of them on our hands. Fortunately, Charlotte assured me that there really *are* twenty-seven-hole golf courses! They are presented in three sets of nine holes each: The Front Nine, The Back Nine, and The Third Nine. Generally, one only plays two groups of nine on any given round or day for a total of eighteen, but this format allows for greater variety of play on the same course.

So twenty-seven holes it was for us – and that's also why we refer to our chapters here in this book as "Holes" instead of chapters. And yes, to be *completely* accurate, we *do* have a twenty-eighth chapter here…but we call that one *"The Real 19ᵗʰ Hole,"* and it's considered sort of a *bonus*, an epilogue kind of a chapter; so we feel our twenty-seven hole concept remains relatively intact!

It was always our intention that this book should be *"not for golfers only"*; hopefully, we have hit the right balance between presenting enough golf-centered material to keep the golfers happy, and also presenting enough descriptive and generalized material that the non-golfers will find the references interesting as well. We almost always use golf concepts as metaphors for life in general, and as you'll see, the timeless teachings and wisdom of *A Course in Miracles* readily apply to everything we may ever encounter in life, on and/or off of the golf course.

One thing we should mention here is the Course's use of the term "God" throughout its teachings (and ours as well.) For any readers who might be put off by this, perhaps due to some previously encountered difficulties with the way God had been presented in the past…well, as you'll quickly see, both ACIM and AGCIM present an understanding of God as a totally loving, completely supportive, and entirely non-judgmental creative power; not as some bearded old man in the sky, looking down on us with critical judgment, ready to punish us severely for any and all infractions. God, as the Course understands God, is the being and power that created us, sustains us, and loves us *(all of us)* infinitely, eternally, and completely – so in God, there is absolutely nothing to fear!

A Course in Miracles is an interesting body of work, in that it is freely available from a variety of sources, particularly over the Internet; but it is also and perhaps best known in its printed forms, the venerable *Second Edition* and, more recently, the *Third Edition*, which contains additional supplemental writings in conjunction with the original material. Those editions of the Course are published by the *Foundation for Inner Peace* and are copyrighted by the *Foundation for A Course in Miracles*. The authors of this book support and endorse the efforts of both of those Foundations in presenting and preserving the accuracy and integrity of *The Course*. We heartily encourage our readers to seek out and use those editions of ACIM for their ongoing study and practice of *A Course in Miracles*, just as we do ourselves.

A Golf Course in Miracles is not the kind of book that needs to be read in one continuous flow. It *can*, to be sure; but it can also certainly be read a little here, a little there, as it is in many ways a series of essays on various topic areas of golf, and life, and the nature of the universe itself. It is intended to be light-hearted, even humorous at times, and certainly uplifting, motivational, and inspiring throughout. We hope you will find these to be your impressions as you read the book!

Rather than attempt to identify which one of us is writing any particular element of AGCIM, we are following one simple formula for the entire book: in each individual Hole/chapter, Charlotte's writing will come first, and my writing will follow. It should be fairly obvious which one of us is "speaking" at any given point, anyway…but following this simple arrangement should help to avoid the likelihood of any confusion.

It is the wish of both your authors that you will find this book to be a valuable companion in bringing an added element of joy, peace, and inspiration into your life. Hopefully, a lot of golfers will now discover something about *A Course in Miracles* – and hopefully a lot of Course students will discover that they are now interested in golf! It is our sincere hope and prayer that *everyone* who reads this book will come away with a smile on his/her face, and a greater sense of lightness and love in their heart.

So, with a phrase that my lovely wife Helen suggested to Charlotte and me, to be used as we "tee off" on our journey into *A Golf Course in Miracles:*

"Let's get swinging!"…shall we?

Prelude

*by **Charlotte McGinnis***

Once upon a time, we were in ***Golf Heaven***. Once upon a time, we knew only pars, birdies, and eagles. Once upon a time, golf courses were maintained perfectly. The greens were smooth and true, the fairways were manicured so each shot would set up as if on a tee, and the bunkers were always raked and smooth. Also, there were no toxic chemicals used to keep the courses green!

Everyone was happy while playing their rounds of golf, and they loved and encouraged all of their partners on the course. Your shots all landed exactly where you intended them to go every time. There was no need for competition because everyone was playing his/her optimum game! Life *and* golf, needless to say, were good!

One afternoon, while having drinks and conversation in the club-house, (which was also just as perfect as the course), the question arose: *What would it be like to play a round of golf and miss a shot?* From that insane question, many other questions were asked. What would it be like to play on a chemical laden golf course? How would it feel to play in extreme heat or cold? How about if you did not to-tally love and appreciate who you were playing with? Before long, everyone had questions, everyone was curious.

When everyone got into their Lexus golf carts to go back to their beautifully appointed luxury homes, standing in the middle of the gold laden cart path was the Director of Golf, inviting everyone to come to a meeting with the ***"Big Gal!"*** (In Golf Heaven, GOLF was an acronym for **G**od, **O**neness, **L**ove, and **F**orgiveness, and we were all extensions of that knowing.)

At the meeting, God shared with the group that She had overheard the conversations at the clubhouse and was intrigued. She said to the group, "You know what? I would love to allow each of you the opportunity to experience duality. I think it could be such a gift to see your brothers and sisters as separate from yourself, and each of you could have the experience of hitting a shot out of a divot in the fairway, a footprint in the sand, or putt over an unrepaired ball mark on the green."

And then She said, "*Go for it!* Have a ball. But remember it is only a dream. Although it is impossible to be separate from me and from each other, in your dream, you can make up anything you want! In your dream, you have free will to listen to the voice of your higher self – or that of your ego. Your higher self, or the Holy Spirit within you, will instantly make you aware of my presence; the ego is the little *'devil'* on your shoulder that wants to '**E**dge **G**od **O**ut!' Not to worry, that little ego has no power over you or me, but in the dream, he can make your rounds of golf and life *seem* pretty miserable."

So God waved her Big Bertha over us all and allowed us to sleep. When we woke up, we said to our parrot, *"Birdie…I don't think we are at St. Andrews anymore!"*

Immediately, you ran to the local municipal course and walked up to the first tee ready to tee it up, and all of a sudden a gentleman came running up asking for your tee time and receipt. "What are a tee time and a receipt?" you asked. This was just the beginning; once you got that settled, the three other players in your group were miserable. They cussed and slammed their clubs to the ground and were not the least bit supportive of you and your round.

You then looked around to notice that there were no women on the course. You asked the fellows you were playing with, "Where are the women golfers?" They laughed and said, "We don't allow broads on the course before noon!" And even more surprising, the acronym for GOLF was no longer **G**od, **O**neness, **L**ove, and **F**orgiveness, but rather **G**entleman **O**nly, **L**adies **F**orbidden!

"Where am I?" you asked. The people are not so nice, the courses are difficult, and you need a tee time to play! But then you remembered…the last words out of God's mouth before you went to sleep…*"My child, do not be afraid, you will see such despair and toxicity on the golf courses in your dreams, but remember you are asleep."*

All you have to do is click your Foot Joys together three times and say: *"I can choose pars instead of this!"*

And so the dream continues…

How long you choose to play here is up to you!

THE FRONT NINE

Hole 1

"I Need Par Nothing!"

(Inspired by A Course in Miracles: *Text-18.VII)*

"I need do nothing."

You are reading this, thinking to yourself, I need par nothing? Isn't that the goal of every golfer, to match par on every hole, or at least on some of them, depending on where you are with your game? Please, don't stop reading just yet and send the book back for a refund…it gets better! I invite you to explore each chapter with an open mind and consider the lessons discussed so that you may enjoy the game of golf more, and have a richer experience both on and off the course!

The human experience is based upon meeting par, or exceeding it to feel as though we are worthy. We spend countless hours on the driving range, seeking to find that "missing link" that will enable us to finally have some control over the outcome of our shots, reaching the green in regulation, and then tapping in a short putt for par. Oh, it feels *soooo* good! Life is grand and we feel great! Par is a wonderful thing. Having goals and achieving them is fantastic! But what about if that dreaded bogey, or worse yet, double or triple bogey shows up, is life still so wonderful?

In truth, yes! Your score need not have any impact on your ability to enjoy the game. We are so programmed to base our happiness on external circumstances. Birdie, feel great! Par, feelin' pretty good. Bogey, OK, I can live with that. Double bogey, triple bogey… *yuck!* You are ready to heave the clubs into the lake, stomp your feet and whine like a baby, and more than that, you feel awful! Sound familiar?

I invite you to open up to the possibility that you can enjoy your experience on the course regardless of your score. It has been said that we have many more imperfect shots than perfect ones in a round of golf. Once the emotions of negativity, anger, and dismay take hold of you, you have lost control. The feelings rushing through your body will set the stage for the next shot. Feelings of anger, frustration, and failure are certainly not the energy you want to carry with you. Why? Because they create tension in the body, and as golfers, you must know by now, tension is not conducive to a good golf swing.

Emotional Intelligence is necessary for success in everything. When you are able to manage your emotions, you are in control. You are not being taken over by the demons of stress! On the golf course, or in life, those who attain success and mastery in life are those who are able to manage their emotions when circumstances are not so cordial.

I suggest that if you have not executed a perfect shot, step back, take a breath, and say to yourself: *"Interesting."* "Interesting" takes the charge out of the perceived judgment that you have made and enables you to move forward in a more peaceful and composed manner. You are more relaxed and able to execute the next shot or hole with a clearer mind. *Mastery* is not needing conditions to be a certain way for you to feel whole. *Mastery* is being detached, becoming an observer of life without judgment, and enjoying the journey.

Whether you are parring every hole or not, peace is a choice that you can make. The irony is, once you are able to be happy regardless of the outcome, your shots will come with ease, you will enjoy the game more, and you will create a space for pars and birdies to come abundantly!

"I need par nothing." Your worth is established by God, and there is nothing you can do to change it. Take a moment and reflect on this thought. You are perfect and there is no score that will make you more perfect or less perfect. What others think of you is none of your business. What *you* think of you is all that matters! There is so much power and freedom in accepting this truth for yourself.

Does this mean that you should not aspire to play better? What about wanting to refine your swing? On the contrary – as spiritual beings, having a human experience, we are meant to create. We can always be and do better. The difference is that you no longer are *needing* to be and do better to feel worthy, because you already are!

It takes so much energy to resist the flow of all the good that wants to come your way, and so little energy to step into the flow of life. Life is not meant to be a struggle. We are here to experience only good. The thoughts you choose are creating the feelings in your body. Choose the thoughts that make you feel good! Then the great shots, eagles, birdies, and pars will come flying your way!

It is my favorite line from *A Course in Miracles*. Now I will admit that I have many favorite lines from the Course; in fact, for me, the book is filled with favorite lines! But *"I need do nothing"* seems to have an unusually high degree of both relevance and resonance in my case. It also picks up slightly different variations of meaning, depending on which words are emphasized within the phrase itself.

If we say, "I need do ***nothing***," we focus on the fact that we're not talking about just doing some things but not others; we are talking about needing do *nothing* at all. If we say, "I need ***do*** nothing," the emphasis changes to our need to not "act" all the time, to develop that *Mastery Mindset* that Charlotte presents so eloquently in her *Zen Golf* teaching – to simply "allow," and be what we are and as we are, without compulsion.

And when we say the phrase as, "I ***need*** do nothing," we get into my personal territory. As someone who generally feels as if things are going to fall completely apart if I'm not actively involved in every aspect of each and every thing at all times…it has become abundantly clear to me that this message from the Course is directed *straight at me* when it tells me loud and clear, "Gene, you ***need*** do nothing!"

Now, of course, we are not expected to actually do nothing at all while we still seem to be here on Earth. How could we? We still have bodies to feed and care for, loved ones to look after, jobs to tend to, and golf courses to attempt to conquer. What *A Course in Miracles* is telling us is that we want to develop a mindset wherein we know that while we *seem* to be in this world, *we are not of it*. We, as perfect creations of God, are ultimately (and in truth) unaffected by what appears to happen here, no matter how "serious" it may seem to be from an Earthly perspective. Even Yoda understood this, when he said, "Luminous beings are we, not this crude matter," in one of the Star Wars movies. *(You know, perhaps Charlotte will begin teaching "Jedi Golf" sometime in the future. I imagine she'll use a light-saber rather than a 9-iron!)*

This essential concept applies to *everything* we seem to encounter, from a hangnail to a heart attack, from a financial meltdown to a flicked finger from a disgruntled driver. In ultimate truth, there is nothing we need ever do. So how do we handle the discrepancy between what seems to happen here on Earth, and what is actually the reality of who and what we truly are? And what the heck does any of this have to do with making par?

Well, as Charlotte has already alluded to, the game of golf, in many ways, can be seen as a metaphor for life. And meeting par or making (or exceeding) par is a wonderful metaphor for what we all deal with every day: "making the grade," being good enough, and smart enough...*and gosh darn it, having people like us!* But all kidding aside, this is precisely what the Course is addressing in this teaching, and what we are presenting in this chapter of *A Golf Course in Miracles*. We all need to come to the understanding that, as perfect, eternal creations of God, there is nothing we need to do that has not already been done, and nothing we need to acquire that we do not already have.

So how do we handle the apparent demands and requirements of life? People always ask me, "How do we maintain a *Course in Miracles* mindset while dealing with the 'needs' of the world?" Well, as my buddy Gary Renard likes to say when answering this question in our podcasts together: *"Don't be weird!"* Just be normal. Do what "normal" people seem to do in this world: eat, sleep, bathe *(we hope!),* play golf, earn money, spend money, look out for the happiness and well being of yourself and others. But at the same time, know (and continue to learn) that we are not *of* this world, not really. And in our true reality, there is truly nothing we need, nothing we need do...and no hole we need par!

Hole 2

"My drive holds only
what I swing with God."

(Inspired by A Course in Miracles: Workbook *Lesson 141-Review IV)*

"My mind holds only what I think with God."

A Course in Miracles teaches that we are living in a dream. In this dream, we believe that we are separate, and we believe that we are worthy only when we accomplish that which we think will make us feel adequate. Our ego mind is always looking for something that will make us feel good, and believe me, a 275-yard drive down the center of the fairway feels pretty darn good! Having been a golf professional for over thirty years, I have personally experienced and witnessed the experience of "paralysis by analysis!" The ego mind is constantly wanting to find the "next thing" that will be the answer to all of your problems. You watch the golf instructors on TV, order devices from the Internet, and take endless lessons, all with the great hope of curing that dreaded slice, or help you to gain more distance!

Before you know it, you are worse off than when you started! What happened? I am by no means devaluing any of these things, but I am suggesting that these may not be the total answer to your prayers. To do anything well, you must have a quiet mind. You need to listen to your higher self – your "inner self."

When I was a competitive player, I played by feel. I understood how cause and effect worked to produce the shots I was choosing to create and I had an empty mind. I also had many lessons along the way. At each lesson, I would implement the ideas suggested by the pro I was working with, and used my intuition and feel to find a way to make it work for me. As a result, I was a pretty good player. In 1988, I was teaching golf at a country club in the PGA Metropolitan Section of New York. Each year, I would attempt to qualify for the U.S. Women's Open with the dream of one day making it! The qualifying tournament that year was in New Jersey and I was, as always, looking forward to showing up and giving it my best shot. Although I had not been working on my game at all, I had confidence in my abilities – and I qualified! I was going to tee it up the next week with the "big girls!" Needless to say, I was thrilled!

I was playing the next day with a fellow professional who at the end of the round made the statement, *"I can't believe you made it to the U.S. Open with that golf swing!"* I was crushed! The next week preparing for the Open, I worked hard to show up with a "better swing." I changed my grip, stance, and swing so much that I had no idea what I was doing. By the time I got to Baltimore, I could not get the ball airborne! What happened? How could I have lost my confidence and the swing I had developed and nurtured for over twenty years in only a week? What happened was that I began thinking so much about my swing, I lost all feel for the game. I was paralyzed! A painful experience yes, but what a powerful lesson! I learned at that moment that I had to work with my students within the framework of *their* feel and understanding. I became a better student *and* teacher of the game.

The same holds true with the lesson "My mind holds only what I think with God." You have so much wisdom and power within your own mind and yet you are so willing to give it away! The power and wisdom of God is *in* you! Does that mean that you stop taking lessons and buying swing aids? No, not at all. I am suggesting, however, that you listen to your inner guide. Ask yourself, does this feel right for me? If not, communicate to your instructor, "This does not make sense to me," or "This does not feel right!" Your golf professional is your partner, and should be willing to work with you and listen to you. If not, maybe you should find a new teacher! Had I known then what I know now, I most likely would have responded to the comment, *"How did you make it to the U.S. Open with that golf swing?"* with a simple answer: ***"Thank you for sharing..."***— and moved on!

There is a statement in *A Course in Miracles*: *"A universal theology is impossible, but a universal experience is not only possible but necessary."* What that means is that we are all seeking the same experience, the experience of GOD, but there are many different paths to getting there. In choosing your perfect teacher/partner, you need to find the one that is a fit for you. Pay attention to your "gut feeling," for that is where God is! When you do this, you cannot fail!

In golf, your drive is what really gets things underway. In fact, the first drive on the first hole is truly the beginning of the entire game. In *A Golf Course in Miracles*, we are continuously presenting golf as a metaphor for life; and in that sense, your drive – the opening of your golf game – is very much like "getting out of bed" each day, the start of a new round, the beginning of another day of life here on this dream-planet known as Earth.

How do we want to start each drive, or each day, then? Since there is a thought that precedes every action, let's take a look at the nature of thought, especially as *A Course in Miracles* discusses it. The Course distinguishes between the thoughts we think with our ego mind, which are ultimately unreal…and the thoughts we think "with God," which are our true thoughts. This is not just a subtle distinction! Far from it: It is the very cornerstone of the Course's teaching, and the concept that will ultimately set us free from all illusion, and all belief in separation from our Source.

"My mind holds only what I think with God." The key word here is, *"only."* My mind – my *real* mind, not the ego mind – holds only the thoughts that I think, and, therefore, share, with God. Those are my real thoughts; all the rest is simply ego-chatter. We are constantly seeming to straddle those two thought systems, and we can only serve one master at a time. We are, at every instant, thinking either with the ego, and sharing its thoughts, or we are thinking with God, and sharing God's thoughts. (And guess which thought system brings us happiness and peace…and maybe even a better golf swing?)

When *A Golf Course in Miracles* states, *"My drive holds only what I swing with God,"* we mean it! My drive – my *real* drive – truly holds only what I swing with God. The ego's drive, if I choose to think with the ego, is filled with doubt and fear: *"Will I hook? Will I slice? Will I shank the dang ball?"* Another dose of anxiety with every swing… Lucky for us all, *those* drives are not even real!

My real drive is the one I swing with God. And even though the drive itself (as part of a game of golf here on Earth) is not technically "real," if I see that drive as part of a thought I am sharing with God, my **experience** of it can happily reflect reality! Confidence, peace, unlimited joy, and unattachment to the outcome, **whatever** seems to happen as a result of my action, I am totally happy with the way things turn out.

And that really swings, baby! When we can be completely "in the moment," thinking with the quiet mind that we share with God, listening to the higher self, the inner self, the inner guide that Charlotte describes – in that mindset, we can find a better drive on every hole, a better life each and every day…and a happier and more peaceful outcome for every situation that ever presents itself to us – on the golf course, or anywhere else we seem to be!

Hole 3

"No fairway I see means anything."

(Inspired by A Course in Miracles: Workbook *Lesson 1)*

"Nothing I see...means anything."

"Nothing I see means anything." *Hmmm...*what a ridiculous idea! This is when students of *A Course in Miracles* have been known to throw the book across the room, in the trash can, or give up studying the Course altogether! Actually, this is where things get really interesting; this statement is the beginning of the undoing of your limited thinking!

A Course in Miracles teaches that we give everything all the meaning that it has for us. If that is the case, then where does this meaning come from? Quite simply, *the past.* We have all been programmed to see things from the perspective of things we have experienced or learned from others' experiences from the past. To mention a few:

31

our family, religious doctrine and dogma, and the constant bombardment of the media.

From a scientific perspective, our universe is made up of tiny particles of energy. This energy is constantly changing based on the energy we project upon it. Our energy field is responding to our thoughts. When we are choosing thoughts that make us feel good, or thoughts that make us feel afraid, that will be our experience. When we are projecting the energy of fear and limitation, then that is what will be reflected back to us. When we are projecting feelings of confidence and well being, that will be reflected back to us as well.

So, where does, "No fairway I see means anything" fit into your golf game? Let's say, for example, you have a particular hole that you have played several times, and every time you have played it, you have not played it well. Fairway? What fairway! You have spent more time in the woods looking for your ball and chopping your way out, than on any fairway! You approach this hole each time you play and where does your mind go? Most likely to the woods, exactly where you do not want to hit your drive! Energy follows thought and if your thoughts are "in the rough," where do you think your shot is going?

The more beneficial practice for a successful shot would be to start creating your game before you get onto the golf course. This is a form of visualization and will prove to be quite helpful for future success.

Find a quiet spot free of distractions, where you are comfortable. Take a few deep breaths with your eyes closed, and gently release any mind chatter that may be going on in your mind. Take yourself to the course where you are playing your next round of golf. Envision yourself on the first tee gently gazing down the fairway. How would you like to play this hole? Where would you like to see your drive land. How about your next shot, your putts… While practicing your round in your mind, allow the *feelings* of successful shots into your body. ***Feelings*** are our most creative source. Feelings of success bring forth success; feelings of failure bring forth failure.

Take time to go through your entire round, envisioning and *feeling* your perfect game. This practice will enable you to release the past fears you have projected onto a fairway or hole and enable you to create a new and more enlightened experience.

*You may have difficulty at first with this practice. Eighteen holes in your mind may not happen at first. Do what you are able to in the beginning and continue to practice this exercise as often as you can; you will be amazed at the results!

"No fairway I see means anything." We need to practice our swing on the range before we have the confidence to take it on the course. To implement these ideas, we need to spend time developing the mental game also.

As you become a conscious creator of your experience on the course, you are no longer a victim of your past memories; you are now creating new meaning in the present moment. Congratulations, you are now in the Zone!

The fairway is to golf what the prairie was to the expansion of the American West, what the ocean is to our planet, what "outer space" is to the solar system; it is the vast, open, empty space between where we are at the moment, and where we intend to go.

Pretty daunting concept, isn't it? I can't help but think of those incredible images from the movie *Apollo 13*, where we saw that little, tiny space capsule moving alone through the void. That isolated,

33

vulnerable little pocket of protection which was keeping the astronauts inside of it alive, as it made its way through the vastness of that empty, inherently dangerous vacuum of space.

Imagine how that little golf ball feels, being violently shot off the safety of its tee, and into the open void of that immense fairway. Kind of makes you feel sorry for the little guy, doesn't it?

But in all seriousness, our thoughts about a fairway encompass a number of these elements. The size of it! The openness, the sheer dimensions of it can be staggering. And *anything* can happen; you can end up too far right, too far left, too short, in a bunker, or even miss the cursed fairway entirely, as big as it is! Wow, all of that worry, all of that concern, all of those possibilities to account for... it sure must mean a lot, right?

Wrong! *No fairway I see means anything*. Why? The answer can be found within the lesson of *A Course in Miracles* (in fact, the very first, Lesson 1) from which we were inspired: ***"Nothing I see... means anything."*** The actual ACIM lesson develops the thought further, stating, *"Nothing I see in this room (on this street, from this window, in this place) means anything."* We could add to that, *"On this fairway,"* or for that matter, anywhere else that might come to mind.

How can this be, that nothing means anything? Well first off, to get all *Matrix* on you (in that film, the character *Neo* learns, *"There is no spoon",*) it is because here in our example, ***"There is no fairway!"*** But understanding that there does *seem* to be a fairway in front of us, how can it – or anything else – not mean anything?

We learn the "rest of the story" about this in the second lesson from *A Course in Miracles*: *"I have given everything I see in this room (on this street, from this window, in this place) all the meaning it has for me."* From *A Golf Course in Miracles* perspective, the reason

34

that no fairway I see means anything is because *"I have given this fairway all the meaning it has for me."*

Charlotte has explained this very clearly by stating that this meaning comes from the past. All of our past experiences with fairways – the good shots, the bad shots, all of the possible outcomes to every shot we have ever made before – all of that is what we think we see when we look at a fairway. But none of that addresses what we see ***now!*** (And none of that addresses the fact that the fairway isn't even *there*, in reality…but that's for another discussion.) The point being made here is that all of these ego-based thoughts about the past, about previous failures, about all of the things that could possibly go wrong with this fairway shot I'm about to make…all of those thoughts can only keep me from making the best possible shot I can right now, right at this moment.

The ball is right in front of you, before you take that shot. The ball will only be in one place after the shot, irrespective of how large and imposing that fairway appears to be. So what does all that "open space" really matter? When we can see that both we and the ball can only seem to be in one place at a time, and the ball is going to go exactly where it is directed to go – especially when we remember that, *"My drive holds only what I swing with God"* – then why should we be in the slightest way concerned about all of that open space in front of us, as long as we continue to remember that *"No fairway I see means anything!"*

Hole 4

"I do not know what any club is for."

(Inspired by A Course in Miracles: Workbook *Lesson 25)*

"I do not know what anything is for."

When I was playing and teaching golf for a living, I would sometimes play a round of golf with only a few clubs. Usually a fairway wood, 7-iron, wedge, and a putter. The interesting thing that happened was that I would shoot around the same score that I would with my full set of fourteen clubs! I was not alone in that experience; whomever I would play with at the time had the same outcome.

Over my thirty years as an instructor, I have introduced thousands of men, women, and children to the game. Golf, unlike any other sport, has many components. There are usually at least four sets of tees on each hole; every golf course is different, based on the terrain and climate of the area. The conditions are never the same, pin locations on the greens change daily, and there are fourteen clubs to execute in a round of play.

With any new golfer, it is usually quite a while before it becomes necessary to use all of the tools in the bag. And for many, I find it best to limit the number of clubs used for a new player. From my personal experience, playing with three or four clubs instead of the full set usually did not hinder my round.

Technology in golf is changing at warp speed. Golf balls are flying farther than ever before, clubs are designed to be more forgiving and produce more distance, and the teaching industry has become so technical that many students, (at all levels) are leaving lessons more confused than when they started.

I would entertain the questions asked by my students about the latest tip they heard on the television or on the Internet. Many of them would show up at their lesson smiling ear to ear with the newest gadgets wanting me to give them my "seal of approval!" I would engage them in their enthusiasm, while quietly chuckling to myself, thinking that they were missing the point. All of this wonderful technology, and yet handicaps overall have not improved for golfers.

I fell in love with the game of golf when I was seven years old. My father would take my sisters, brother, and me to the driving range and to the miniature golf course and we loved it! With his 30 handicap, he would give my sister and me *"tips"* on how to swing the club. Both of us became single digit players when we were in our early teens in spite of our *"lessons"* and *"sub-standard"* equipment. How did we manage to accomplish this? In all fairness, we eventually received excellent instruction and were provided with clubs that were considered good at the time, but we had a very strong foundation and confidence even before our first lessons.

My opinion is that we had "empty minds." Our swings were not paralyzed by over thinking and analyzing every point of where the club was in our swing. I had no idea really *"what any club was for!"* I knew the driver went the farthest, and the putter was used on the putting green. I had a strong sense of the "inner game" before I knew what the "inner game" was! With that, I developed feel and creativity on the course. When I study the pros and greats of the past with those of today, I have noticed that creativity and imagination on the course is not as prevalent today as it was years ago. Sam Snead, Arnold Palmer, Jack Nicklaus, and the golfers of an earlier era, created "magic" on the course. Not to say that the players of today don't, but based on equipment of the past and the technology of today...the game of today is a different animal.

It seems as though I may not have an appreciation for technology and advancements in the game. Not true. However, I do know the value of simplicity and an empty mind. I seek balance between the two. I take advantage of the technology of equipment and instruction, but I also suggest that students of the game take time to pay attention to what is going on inside themselves! Integrating technology with the "inner game" is where our best golf exists!

When many of you read the heading of this chapter, "I do not know what any club is for," and wonder what the heck that means, I invite you to be willing to develop a stronger sense of the wealth of internal knowledge that you possess. You may want to take only three or four clubs out on the course with you and pay attention to what is happening. When you play a round with only a few clubs, what do you have to do to get the job done? You will begin to see, that you will let go of the past meanings and ideas of what each club is used for, and "find another way" to play. This practice will teach you how to develop creativity on the course and eventually will give a whole new meaning to what the clubs in your bag are "needed" for.

Where in life have you lost your creativity? Have you given your power to technology and analyzing things too much? Our "instant gratification" society, although wonderful for many of its gifts it offers us, has also created a dependency on external "fixes" or

39

"cures" to just about anything we could ever think we need. This dependency has made it unnecessary to go inside ourselves and figure things out. We have gotten lazy. We have lost our ability to create.

Everything in our universe is neutral, and we give everything all the meaning it has for us. Within you are so many treasures you have not yet uncovered because you have allowed the "external world" to dictate your experience. Your experiences on the golf course and in life are a projection of your beliefs. There is nothing in the world that can touch what is inside of you! Now that you are becoming aware, you have the power to choose differently! Golf will never be the same for you, because you are becoming more present, and free of the past. As you master these techniques, you will master your game, and your life!

The most basic explanation for this chapter title from *A Golf Course in Miracles* known as "Hole 4" comes once again right out of the Hollywood movies, courtesy of our favorite *Matrix* golf guru, Neo Nicklaus: Why do I not know what any club is for? Because, *"there is no club."* I mean, if the universe is just an illusion, then this golf club is an illusion, too…therefore, it's not really *here*, so *there is no club!* Simple!

But once again, we realize that we do *seem* to be here, and there does seem to be that club in our hand…so what is it for? From a purely practical and golf-centric perspective, there are different clubs for different shots and different circumstances. Charlotte has beautifully explained much of the basic theory regarding club selection. But her larger, and much more essential point is the one that deals with the "empty mind," the *beginner's mind*, that open mind that enables one to approach a situation – or a golf shot – without any pre-conceived solutions getting in the way of a chance to tackle a new challenge with complete creativity and openness.

There is a terrific story, which you may have already heard, about a businessman who seeks out a certain legendary spiritual master in remote Asia, and upon meeting him, begins to tell him all that he has studied and learned. They sit together, and the businessman goes on and on about all of his experiences, while the master is pouring tea…and he continues pouring even when the cup begins to over-flow onto the man's lap! The man looks up in astonishment as the master says, *"This tea cup is like you. You are so full of what you know, there is no room for anything else to be allowed in."*

Generally, this story does not go on to reveal that the businessman ended up suing the guru for his dry-cleaning bills! *(I'm kidding!)* But seriously, the real lesson here is that the true master understands that knowing what we do **not** know, and realizing that while in human form, it is impossible to truly know the best outcome in every situation, is the mindset where real breakthroughs and advancement can begin.

Now this doesn't mean that we should not use our valuable experi-ence when making decisions, on or off the golf course. If a 9-iron has always worked well for you on the type of shot that you're fac-ing at the moment, experience would tell you it's a pretty good bet for you to go with that same club once again. But here is the key word in this chapter's teaching: "I do not **know** what any club is for"—*"know,"* meaning absolutely and beyond question. Having experience is wonderful, and a valuable asset, but understanding that experience is just a tool, and not a rule, is the key to maintain-ing that all-important *open mind* that can lead us to new and more creative solutions to any problems we are facing…and any others that may come up down the road.

(And I like that line: ***"It's just a tool, not a rule!"*** Perhaps there's a bumper-sticker business opportunity in my future.)

41

A Course in Miracles Lesson 25, *"I do not know what anything is for"* begins with the statement, "Purpose is meaning." *Anything* will remain ultimately meaningless to us if we do not understand its purpose, if we don't know what it is *really for.* Is this particular golf club meant to achieve a certain loft angle, or cause the ball to travel a certain distance, or provide a bit more back-spin on the landing... *Or is it something else* – the simplest and most likely way to get the ball from point A to point B? And seeing it that way, do I really **know** that this club is the best choice in this instance, or will an open mind allow me to possibly experience a better, happier, and more beneficial outcome by choosing again?

In life, as in golf, experience, education, and practice are all important and valuable assets to develop and maintain within our mental tool kits, utility belts, and golf bags. But perhaps even more valuable is the ability to remain *"open,"* open to new ideas, new techniques, new possibilities. When we can fully embrace the idea that no matter how much we may have learned, we still do not completely **know** what any club – or any **thing** – is for, we find ourselves consistently open to welcoming new possibilities for anything and everything we choose to do.

And that is where **real** mastery begins!

Hole 5

"I tee nothing as it is now."

(Inspired by A Course in Miracles: Workbook *Lesson 9)*

"I see nothing as it is now."

A Golf Course in Miracles is based on the teachings of *A Course in Miracles.* In the ACIM book, there are many core lessons that are presented in different ways. The teachings have been described as being "circular," meaning the themes are recurring. Now that I have made my disclaimer about why it may seem like you are reading the same message over and over again, I want to say, I am not sorry! Although it would be wonderful if we read or heard an idea and got it, very few do. Repetition is a law of learning.

Think about when you are taking a lesson. The pro will tell you to set up a certain way, swing on plane, or maintain balance. You go back for your next lesson, and the lesson was almost the same as the last one. Why? Because you haven't mastered it yet. The same holds true here. When you have accomplished mastery in your life and on the course, your learning is complete. If you are a master, please call me and share your wisdom with me!

"I tee nothing as it is now." Lesson 9 in *A Course in Miracles*, is "I see nothing as it is now." Incidentally, there are 365 lessons in the Course, which are designed to undo and replace our old thought patterns of fear and limitation and replace them with thoughts of love and empowerment. Love, not based on conditions, but rather love based on unconditional acceptance of what is. When we are able to release our "judgments" and be willing to ask for a "miracle," which is simply defined as a "shift in perception," we see the perfection in everything. Peace is no longer based on conditions, but rather our decision and desire to see things differently.

Lesson 1 states: "Nothing I see in this room means anything." The lessons progress to Lesson 9, which is "I see nothing as it is now." In between Lessons 1 and 9, the Course suggests that we see nothing as it is because we are seeing only the past. When you are on the tee, you have a choice, to be fully present in the moment, free of limitations and past failures and successes, and show up with an empty mind. The tee is new, the hole looks different, you see possibilities, and you have created a space of unlimited potential. In this space, also known as the "zone," you are more relaxed, you are the master of the shot you are choosing to make, and success is yours for the making!

I have been a student and teacher of *A Course in Miracles* for thirty years. I have also been a golf professional since 1980. When I teach the Course or when I am giving a golf lesson, I always refresh the basics: grip, alignment, stance, and posture. Swing path, tempo, and balance are always the key issues I address. The same holds true with my spiritual teachings; I get back to basics. Your ego is always wanting to devalue the power of basics, in golf and in life. Your higher self is always seeking simplicity and peace. Humility is necessary for enlightenment…are you willing to be humble in your life and on the course?

44

Taking Lesson 9 from *A Course in Miracles, "I see nothing as it is now,"* and transmuting it into our "Hole 5" in *A Golf Course in Miracles, "I **tee** nothing as it is now,"* actually addresses the parallel between what we see, and what we appear to put into action. The two concepts are inextricably linked, as far as our seeming to be "in the world" is concerned. Even simply "seeing" something – just observing it – is, in effect, an action of a sort. Observing is still doing, albeit a passive form of doing so. The point is that while we seem to be here in the world, we are always doing something; even "seeming to not do anything" is a *"doing,"* in that sense.

If this seems confusing to you, you are not alone, *Grasshopper!*

This world is built on confusion. It completely depends on it for its persistence! If we actually had **no** confusion in anything, if we could "know" things as they truly are, this universe would disappear in an instant. This book you are reading, the golf club you may be holding, the tee in front of you that you are about to hit a ball off the top of...even the body through which you appear to be perceiving all of these things... if you had no confusion whatsoever, and could "know" everything as it is in True Reality, then anything that is illusion would be gone, and only Truth would remain.

Wow, we're swinging through some really deep grass here, aren't we? But rather than continue delving into the deeper aspects of what is real and what is not (at least for the moment), let's get back to some semblance of what *seems* real to us right now, and why we are actually not seeing – or teeing – anything as it really is at the moment.

Charlotte has already addressed the "mental" aspect of why we see (and tee) nothing as it is now. It is because we harbor all of these past thoughts: the judgments, previous experiences, and limitations

45

stemming from how something appeared to be in our previous encounters with it. All of that mental clutter keeps us from being fully in the present moment, *"in the zone,"* and capable of giving our all to what we are addressing right now.

But there is also a purely physics-based angle to what the Course is teaching, and what we are presenting here. When we look at something, we are not actually seeing it as it is *right now;* the photons of light that have reflected off its surface had to travel through space, *and time,* prior to reaching our eyes and being perceived by us. It's similar to when we look at the stars in the sky; the light we are seeing now left those stars many years ago. Depending on how many light-years away that particular star (or star system) is, that light we're seeing only now may have been traveling for thousands of years before we perceive it. Even in the case of Earth's own Sun, the light and warmth we enjoy from the Sun is really over eight minutes old before it reaches us. If the Sun were to somehow burn out in an instant, we would still have eight minutes left before things went dark here on Earth. Barely time enough to finish the current hole we're playing! (Of course, that would probably be the least of our worries, in that event.)

But I digress. Granted, the golf ball on the tee in front of us is a lot closer than the Sun, or the stars, or the galaxies far, far away. But the principle is precisely the same: we are not seeing the ball, or the tee – *or anything else we ever perceive* – as it is **now**. We are always seeing an image of what **was**, in a previous instant in time. Whether it was eight thousand years ago, or eight minutes ago, or eight nanoseconds ago, the point is we are not seeing anything **now**. We are always viewing images that were made in the past.

From a pragmatic standpoint, that might seem like a mere technicality: *"Hey, we see what we see, don't we?"* But it gets to the root point about our lack of true perception. We believe that what we're looking at is really there, even though it is always *at best* an image of something in the past. And if we can be convinced that images from the past are our true reality...then what else can we become convinced of?

Once again, the "open mind" that we discussed previously comes into play here. Sure, the image of the ball on the tee is accurate enough for our current purposes. If we can get a decent enough picture of it in our head, we can attempt a decent enough tee shot.

But, if we can also develop a mindset which tells us that everything we seem to see is always an "image that I have made," and that I'm never seeing *anything* exactly as it is right now...how much more open and flexible can we be, and how much more creative and intuitive can we become in our abilities to handle any problems that ever come along – *or,* any tee shots?

Hole 6

"I am upset because I slice a ball that is not there."

(Inspired by A Course in Miracles: Workbook *Lesson 6)*

"I am upset because I see something that is not there."

It's time to have some fun now! If your mind is not spinning yet, give me a chance; it will be! "I am upset because I see something that is not there." In a nutshell, there is nothing "out there." No, you have not stepped into a science fiction movie; you are in reality. *A Course in Miracles* teaches us that we are living in a dream, a dream that seems extremely real. The Eastern traditions refer to this dream as the "illusion." As human beings having a spiritual experience, we are not asked to deny the dream, but rather make choices that reflect our higher consciousness.

The statement, there is nothing "out there," is challenging. Challenging, because from the moment we are born into this world, we are taught to believe that everything is "out there!"

Our life, and golf experience, is given birth by thought. In truth, our thoughts are things, and our thoughts are creating our reality. Negative, fear-based or ego thoughts create feelings, and these feelings are creating your reality. The same holds true with the opposite; positive, loving thoughts create positive and loving feelings in your body, and these feelings are creating a like reality.

As a golfer, a slice is certainly not the most desired shot in the game, unless it is on command for a desired outcome. A sliced ball is a weak shot, which tends to land in a less than desirable spot. Needless to say, slices are not the dream shot of many golfers.

Energy follows thought. You prepare to hit your shot, and a slice appears. The ball is in the water, sand, woods, or other less than desirable place. The slice was not there, until you put it there. You are saying to yourself, why the *he__* would I have chosen a slice? What I wanted was a shot in the middle of the fairway! But the slice happened because you created it!

You are 100 percent responsible for everything in your life. Of course, there are many situations and circumstances that you think you were a victim of, or that you would have never chosen. If you can allow yourself to be a little bit willing to explore this idea more, you will begin to tap into an inner knowing and power like you have never known. There is great strength and comfort in the idea that you have created everything in your life. That means if you created a situation, then you have the power to change it! Did you choose to experience negative situations in your life? Yes, but not necessarily on a conscious level. Most of your decisions and actions are subconscious. The good news is, you can re-program your subconscious mind.

You cannot afford the luxury of a negative thought! Your dominant thoughts are creating your reality. *A Course in Miracles* is described as a course in "mind training." You must train yourself to think differently. Once a negative thought enters your mind, choose again! Choose a better feeling thought. The problem is that when most people have a negative thought enter their mind, they dwell on it, draw in allies, and make up a grand story based on something that isn't even there! Only *you* can change the thoughts that don't serve you. Pay attention! When fear, negativity, and "a slice" enter your mind, choose a different thought, a thought that makes you feel good. Eventually, there will only be room for the thoughts that produce successes, not slices!

I know what you're thinking. *"Oh, here he goes again with another Matrix reference…but this time, instead of 'There is no spoon,' it's going to be, 'There is no ball,' right?"*

Well, yes, I did in fact think that. And even though it is technically true, and further, even though the Heisenberg uncertainty principle might in fact stipulate that the ball we would seem to be observing will never fly in an entirely predictable path and direction anyway… this is not actually where I was going to go with this.

I was going to reference the Lesson from *A Course in Miracles* from which we take the inspiration for our golf instruction: *"I am upset because I see something that is not there."* In this case, the ball that we see, before we slice it (or hook it, or do anything else to it) is not the ball that is actually there. It may just be, as we have discussed earlier, the past image of a ball. Yes, maybe it is this same ball that seems to be in front of you, only seen at some point in time earlier than right "now." But also, perhaps it is an image that represents primarily a *memory* of a ball involved in a past shot – and perhaps even one that we *sliced...?*

Remember, as Charlotte also noted, that we are responsible for everything we seem to project in our experiences. And in that sense, we are generating everything that appears to happen to us in this world, whether it is illusion or not.

Now this seems as good a time as any to bring up the following point, which I consider completely essential to being able to embrace this concept: When we say that *"we are responsible"* for everything we see and experience, we are not necessarily speaking about our "human" selves, the "we" that we generally think of ourselves as being. This was one of the hardest concepts for me to grasp, when I first encountered these teachings. "Hey," I would protest *(and often still do!),* "I don't want any of this lousy stuff to happen to me! In fact, I do everything I can to see to it that it *won't* happen! So don't tell me I'm responsible for it."

Relax! *(I tell that to myself as well, all the time.)* We are not suggesting that you, the human person, are actively causing lousy things to happen to yourself. Now, yes, some people *do* cause lousy things to happen to themselves by engaging in self-destructive activities in life...but that's not what we are talking about here. We're talking about even after doing all the right things – practicing your moves (on the golf course, disco dance floor, or anywhere else), after taking all the right precautions, and after making all the right plans and preparations – things still "go wrong" and turn out badly, often resulting in something which is the complete opposite of our consciously desired outcome.

Our responsibility for this occurs at a subconscious level; it could even be thought of as at a level beyond our own world and dimension. At that level, we made (and simultaneously continue to make) decisions which seem to affect us "here and now" in the material world...which obviously includes the golf course as well. And the "presence" *(for want of a better term)* that we are at that level, created the illusion of the golf ball, as well as the sliced or well-executed shot, in an effort to give us *(as we appear to be here in "this world")* the experience of the results of that shot at this seeming moment in time. The elation we feel at making a killer drive, or the frustration and anger at making a lousy slice...either way, it is this experience that "we" were seeking when we thought that setting things up this way would be a good idea.

So that is where our conscious choice, in the present moment, comes into play. We may not all be Zen masters on the golf course, like Charlotte is *(OK, I'm kidding. Even **she** makes the occasional bad shot... or so I've been told!)*, but we **can** be Zen masters of our own thinking. We can understand that the ball itself is not really there. The slice that the driven ball appears to be taking is not really there either. But our **reaction** to it all can be under our direct and conscious control, right now! And we can understand that *"I am upset because I see something that is not there,"* as well as being upset *"because I slice a ball that is not there."* And why on Earth (or anywhere else) should we choose to experience upset because of something that's not even really there?

Remember our earlier instruction, *"My drive holds only what I swing with God"*? Well, keep that in mind. The part of our mind that thought up and projected the world we seem to see and experience (you can also think of it as a function of our "higher self," or "higher consciousness") is *that part* of our mind that thought slicing a golf ball would be a good idea for us to seem to experience at this moment. *Who are we to argue?* But remember, it is the part of our mind that we choose to think with *right now*, that can always "choose again," and choose to experience *anything* – even an apparently lousy golf shot – as something merely "interesting," and nothing to be seen as a source of upset.

And as a result of that *(or at very least, its happy side-effect)*, we may well discover that once we have changed our minds about any forms of upset having any value to us...we may start seeing *many* things change here in our Earthly experiences: even to the point of seeing a lot of those formerly sliced golf shots now flying beautifully down the middle of the fairway!

Hole 7

"I see only the past (in this sand trap.)"

(Inspired by A Course in Miracles: Workbook *Lesson 7)*

"I see only the past."

I was founder and director of a spiritual education and outreach center in Palm Beach County. Our mission was to educate and inspire men, women, and children to find peace in the most challenging of situations. Our community outreach programs included children who had parents with HIV/AIDS, and intended to help them find hope and healing. We were blessed to have countless volunteers who offered their expertise and services to assist us in our mission. One of my most memorable events was when we offered a workshop for these beautiful children. The workshop was given by a gentleman who showed up with a *"Rainbow Vacuum Cleaner."* What did he do with this *"Rainbow Vac,"* you may be asking yourself? What else? *He played music on it!* It seemed a little off the wall at the time, but his message, which went along with the tones of the "Rainbow Vac," was priceless!

We had the children sit in a circle while they were watching this vacuum troubadour sing songs while creating tones on his "unlikely instrument!" You should have seen the looks on the children's faces; they were priceless! As we observed the children's reactions, we could see that although their lives were in turmoil, and they were dealing with more challenges than any child, or adult for that matter, should have to, their situations at home were more comfortable than "R" and his insane musical musings!

Then the miracle occurred; something shifted. The children became more relaxed and amused and eventually began to enjoy the experience! The message of "R" was that although life was reflecting challenging situations, if the children were able to be present, they could experience peace and joy. "R" encouraged the kids to join him in saying, "goodbye past," bringing them into the "now," which was safe and happy. At first, I have to say that I was a little unsure of the presentation, but it ended well. The children left with a sense of hope and renewed possibilities. They had been given an opportunity to release the past!

I am not suggesting to you that you get out your "Rainbow Vac" and start saying affirmations, but I am offering you the opportunity to consider the possibility of looking at your "sand trap" experiences differently. So many golfers have made a "monster" of the dreaded sand trap. The energy of the fear around sand creates a magnet for the ball to go exactly where you do not want it to go – big lesson, but great opportunity for change. A thought to remember: "What you resist, persists."

Sand is neutral, and has only the meaning that you give it. Release the fear, and your experience will change. You may also want to take a few lessons to learn how to get out of the sand with ease. Sand shots are not difficult, but the mass fear projected upon them has made them a "pit of fear" to many golfers. Next time you are in the sand, say to yourself, "goodbye past," and think of the children whose story I shared with you earlier. In spite of their painful experiences, they were able to find peace. What about you?

I was there at *The Palm Beach Center for Living* (the outreach center that Charlotte referenced) the night that fellow came in with the musical *"Rainbow Vac"* to entertain and enlighten the kids. Char and I still chuckle over the memory of that guy and those wide-eyed kids dancing around in a circle, waving their hands in the air and loudly singing, ***"Goodbye, past!"*** as they went. I don't know if the kids understood the lesson he was attempting to teach (or if *we* really did either), but the image remains one of the cutest and funniest things I've ever witnessed!

The larger point though, is well taken. We do actually see only the past, as we have touched upon already in this book. Both from a physics-based point of view, as well as from a metaphysical one, we see nothing truly in the "now," but only in the past. From the material world perspective, that difference may seem insignificant; what do a few nanoseconds really matter between friends, after all? But from a metaphysical, and even from a ***psychological*** perspective, the difference is significant indeed.

The psychology of this concept is obviously important in dealing with a sand trap *(or any other trap)* here in the physical world. If you are focused on what this kind of trap has done to you in the past, you definitely won't be fully *"in the now"* as you take action to get out of the trap at the moment. And you may well even begin to (or continue to) manifest more traps of this same kind as you move forward in life – which we're guessing is the last thing any of us would want to be doing!

As Charlotte stated, *"Sand is neutral, and has only the meaning that you give it."* Why is a sandy beach a wonderful experience, but a sandy bunker is a big problem? Only because we think of it that way, and only because our past experience would try to tell us this is so. But if we see the sand trap *(or the sandy beach)* purely in the moment of "now," we can assign to it whatever experience we choose. Obstacle or opportunity, joy or misery, Heaven or hell...the choices are always ours, when we remember our eternal option to "choose again."

Metaphysically, the realization that we see only the past is even more deeply powerful. *A Course in Miracles* teaches that this illusory universe *(including all of those spoons, golf balls, and fairways that aren't really there)* is not only illusory in terms of *matter* – the physical material that doesn't actually exist in reality – but also in terms of *time.* The Course tells us that everything within the illusion has already happened; it just *seems* to be unfolding and occurring over a subjectively experienced period of time.

Deep stuff! Yes, I know...but so is the sand we'll find in most bunkers, so let's rake it smooth right now. *The Course* states, in Workbook Lesson 158: *"Time is a trick, a sleight of hand, a vast illusion in which figures come and go as if by magic... For we but see the journey from the point at which it ended, looking back on it, imagining we make it once again; reviewing mentally what has gone by."*

This may all seem a little less intimidating when we realize that science is saying exactly the same thing. Einstein showed, and modern quantum physics continues to prove, that time, space, and matter are all interrelated, and that there are no "absolutes" in any of these; they are all interdependent upon each other for their perceived reality. And when seen from the perspective of the "big bang," an event that took place completely *outside* of time and space as we perceive them *(the big bang can be thought of as the beginning of any form or observation of the illusory experience of time)*, it becomes a lot easier to understand the truth of what the Course is telling us, about why we see only the past.

Now, if we can finally get the *least little bit* comfortable with understanding that we see only the past in the *entire universe*, shouldn't it become just a *little easier still* to embrace the knowledge shared in our instruction here? And then…to more peacefully make a better bunker shot by remembering that *we see only the past in this sand trap*?

(Goodbye, past!)

Hole 8

"My mind is preoccupied with past strokes."

(Inspired by A Course in Miracles: Workbook *Lesson 8)*

"My mind is preoccupied with past thoughts."

I have suggested to many of my students over the years, to practice the art of meditation. A fairly common response to my suggestion is the reply, "I tried meditation; I just can't quiet my mind!" My reply is, "Of course, because you have not trained yourself to do so!"

In today's world, most people have very "busy minds." It's no surprise, since we are constantly being stimulated by external means. Television, the Internet, newspapers and magazines, and forty-plus-hour workweeks, all lend themselves to having a very busy mind. The Buddhists call this the "monkey mind." Regardless of what we choose to call it, our minds are very preoccupied. Our minds are on overload!

We are programmed to be gatherers of information, seekers of the next best thing. Not only are we filling our minds with endless data, we take pride in the fact that we have accumulated this vast amount of knowledge. Again, I suggest balance. Information is literally at our fingertips. Type a few "keywords" into the search engine of your computer and you can acquire knowledge in a nanosecond. What a wonderful time to be alive; we are one button away from knowing the "secrets of the universe!"

Yes, technology is a blessing, but it is also a curse, depending on how we choose to use it. The Buddhist symbol yin/yang represents balance. If you are continually feeding your mind with data and information, yet not taking time to be still and integrate this knowledge, balance cannot exist. When you are not in balance, you are not at peace. When you are not in balance, you are not allowing your "inner knowing" an opportunity to come forth.

"My mind is preoccupied with past strokes." This is just one example of how the "monkey mind" controls our present experience. Meditation is a practice that comes in many forms. The goal of meditation is to quiet the mind and to be present, to be here now. When your mind is preoccupied with past shots, you are bringing the past into the present moment. When your mind is still, you are free to create a new experience.

There are many forms of meditation, and the best one is the one that works for you! For some, it is sitting in a lotus position with your legs crossed, spine erect, and repeating mantras or phrases that bring you back to center. For others, a walk in nature, gardening, or cooking will quiet your mind. Take time to think of where you are most peaceful, where your mind is still, and spend more time in that activity. You may evolve into a desire to pursue a more structured practice that will take your further within. Whatever form you choose, the more you practice, the less you will be preoccupied with past thoughts! This will enable you to be more present with each shot you approach and enable more freedom and success.

Meditation is a practice I highly recommend. It is a powerfully effective way to quiet an over-busy mind, to center and re-focus oneself, and to allow all manner of creative expression (and problem solving solutions) to come through. As my co-author has noted, meditation may come in many forms. Formalized styles of meditation can be quite effective, but simpler methods and techniques can sometimes work very nicely too. Personally, I find that basic, repetitive tasks that occupy only a part of my conscious mind can serve well as platforms for creative results in meditation. Things like washing the dishes, cooking, or taking a shower, which only keep a small portion of my thinking mind engaged, often yield some of my more productive and creative ideas.

Deeper and more transcendent forms of meditation, like *TM (Transcendental Meditation)*, or many types of guided meditations, can bring one into the state of a deeply quiet mind…and can often result in profound and sometimes quite startling experiences! But *all* forms and types of meditation are helpful. As I once told an interviewer on the subject, "There is no *wrong* way to meditate."

The constant *busy-ness* of our modern, technological world can really make a calm, meditative state a difficult thing to achieve. But this is one of the primary reasons why achieving it is so important! The only antidote to *busy-ness* is *calm-ness*, and it is precisely this that meditation provides. The Maharishi Mahesh Yogi, the Indian mystic who widely popularized meditation in the 1960s, said, *"If you are too busy to meditate, you are too busy."* (He also supposedly once said, *"Stop drumming on the back of my meditation chair, Ringo!"* But that's another story.)

The bottom line is, the constant chattering of the *"monkey mind"* is a continuous distraction in our lives, and the prime source of what is our greatest challenge in attempting to achieve a quiet, peaceful mind.

There is an often-repeated quote (which I'll repeat again here) from seventeenth-century French mathematician and philosopher Blaise Pascal, which states: *"All men's miseries derive from not being able to sit in a quiet room alone."* (I don't believe that Pascal ever said anything at all about Ringo.)

"To sit in a quiet room, alone"—the quiet mind instead of the monkey mind. *"Swing through trees! Get bananas! Go, go, go!"* Busy, busy, busy...chattering all the way. And you can bet those tree-swinging primates are often busily thinking about branches they've swung on before, how good that last bunch of bananas tasted, and all the tricks and trades of the monkey business that they have learned and acted on previously. Much of the time, they are preoccupied with past thoughts.

Because of the way our human minds and brains were designed, we have a built-in disposition to focus on the past as a means of trying to redesign the present and influence the future. In Lesson 135, *A Course in Miracles* references our folly when we *"attempt to plan the future, activate the past, or organize the present as you wish."* What a meaningful concept! ***"Activate the past."*** We are literally attempting to bring the past to life, to reactivate it, by our repeated focus upon it.

But even more meaningful for our purposes in this chapter, is the fact that *"My mind is **preoccupied** with past strokes (and past thoughts.)"* **Preoccupied** – we're not just *thinking* about the past, we are preoccupied with it, focused on it to the exclusion of all else.

There is a powerful emotional component to this! And how can we possibly be free to contemplate the issue that is before us right now, in the present moment, and see that issue clearly and with all of our creative powers brought to bear if we are preoccupied with thoughts about the past?

We can learn from the past, and develop valuable skills through experience and practice. But when we can let our emotional attachment to past thoughts go, and release that preoccupation with the past that inevitably distorts and blocks our ability to see things and solve problems in the present moment, we can then truly find ourselves always *in the now*, and able to be *"in the zone."*

You can bet that Ringo was not preoccupied with the past on the night the Beatles first played Shea Stadium! And you should not be preoccupied with past thoughts, either, as you are about to take your next stroke on the golf course – or take action on whatever it is you are about to do in your life.

Hole 9

"My putts do not mean anything."

(Inspired by A Course in Miracles: Workbook *Lesson 10)*

"My thoughts do not mean anything."

My putts do not mean anything? Yeah right! Tell that to any golfer who is standing over a three-foot putt to win the club championship or shoot their all-time best score, or a tour player who has a three-foot putt to win the U.S. Open! They probably would not agree!

Lesson 10 in *A Course in Miracles* states that "My thoughts do not mean anything." A pretty radical statement considering that we are programmed to value and protect our thoughts, and now, the Course is telling us they are meaningless? In the human experience, we have a split mind. Having a split mind, we have the power to choose to align our thoughts with love or fear, success or failure, joining or separation. The idea that our thoughts do not mean anything is expressing to us that our ego thought system has no meaning and will never lead us to peace. We are forever looking for ways to make us feel worthy, special, or set us apart from everyone else. Believing that our external conditions can actually make us happy is a lie that the ego would love for us to believe. The ego is forever fighting for its survival.

Back to the three-foot putt. You are preparing to execute the shot, you are ready to "pull the trigger," and most likely, you are already hearing the cheers from the crowd for your victory! Finally, you are somebody! You have now become a champion! Feels great, as it should. Let's explore the other side of this coin. What if you miss the putt? How do you feel then? Are you still feeling like a winner? Is your self-worth still intact?

There is a part of you that is totally unaffected by whether you make the putt or miss it. Your spirit is neutral and sees and experiences the perfection in all things. When you are able to connect with that part of yourself, your true nature, the game changes. You are able to appreciate all aspects of playing the game. You see the beauty of the course more, you enjoy your playing partners, and you are able to play with a clearer mind and no stress. Why? Because you have let go of expectations.

You may be thinking to yourself, if that is the case, why bother? If all I have to do is accept my round no matter how lousy it is, why should I even practice or spend the time and money to become better? Certainly, a very fair question. We are creative beings and we all want to be and do better in all things. Go for it! Set goals, take the lessons, buy the latest and greatest technology, and spend hours on the range. You will get better and that is fabulous! And fun!

The only difference is that you are playing the game from a different mind. You are surrendering to the experience and allowing your true creative nature to take over. The past negative experiences are gone and you are not motivated by need or fear. *Now* the game gets interesting, and much richer. Simply said, you are opening yourself up to greater possibilities and a higher level of satisfaction, peace, and joy than you can imagine! *Your putts do not mean anything,* and yet they can mean so much more!

The reason your putts do not mean anything is because the putts themselves are meaningless. Oh, sure, the putts can *seem* to be very meaningful, and very important; whether you par, birdie, or bogey a hole as a result of any given putt may change the outcome of the game, or of an entire tournament! So what the heck do we mean by saying that putts do not mean anything?

What we mean is, *the putts themselves* do not mean anything. It is how we *choose to react* to each and every putt that will give the putt all real meaning it will ever have. Think about it; if we execute a lousy putt, we can get all negative about it, and let that emotion ruin the rest of the game for us, and perhaps even allow it to sour us on trying to learn better putting techniques as we progress. And on the other hand, a really good putt might leave us feeling all cocky and over-confident, and as a result of that, we get sloppy on the next hole and miss what should be an easy putt that time around.

Or...we can choose to react differently. To the bad putt, we can see it from the more detached, "observer's" perspective (perhaps while utilizing Charlotte's earlier suggestion to utter a Spock-like comment such as, *"Interesting!"* in place of a more angry invective). And by doing so, we can let the bad putt be simply a reason to examine our game more closely, and perhaps inspire us to practice some more effective putting techniques. The same goes for the "good putt"; we can choose to simply observe it – observe it happily, if we choose to! – but still see it from a detached viewpoint, and not

69

allow it to generate an over-confidence that might negatively affect the next putt we make.

The deeper source for this mindset comes from Lesson 10 in *A Course in Miracles,* which states, *"My thoughts do not mean anything."* The Course explains to us that the reason our thoughts do not mean anything is because they are not our real thoughts.

Whoa! Where are we going with this? If our thoughts are not our real thoughts, what the blazes are they? The answer lies in the understanding that we are, at every instant, either thinking with the mind that we share with the *ego*, or the mind that we share with *Spirit:* the Holy Spirit, God, "The Force"...the name we assign to it doesn't matter. It is that concept of the "higher power" that we are all connected to at all times, and in truth, what it is that we really *are.* This is where the "observer" concept comes in. When we can detach ourselves from the idea of our being stuck in these human bodies, subject to illness, suffering, death – and even *the horror of making a bad putt!* – and instead (and as best we can) merely "observe" whatever it is that seems to be happening to us, at that point we begin to think with Spirit, and not with the ego.

And at that level, we can see that nothing within "the illusion" of the material universe really means anything; it is only how we react to it, how we choose to process the experience of it, that will give anything we appear to experience all the real meaning it will ever have for us. And from that perspective, we can know for sure that our putts do not mean anything in and of themselves, and no matter what their outcome appears to be, we can always choose to ultimately experience nothing but a joyful and peaceful reaction to any putt we make...or to any thought we have!

THE BACK NINE

Hole 10

"God is in every green I see."

(Inspired by A Course in Miracles: Workbook *Lesson 29)*

"God is in everything I see."

There is a line in the introduction to *A Course in Miracles* that states: *"The course does not aim at teaching the meaning of love, for that is beyond what can be taught. It does aim, however, at removing the blocks to the awareness of love's presence, which is your natural inheritance."*

There is *nothing* in this world, a.k.a. our dream of separation, that can compare in the slightest way to the experience of God. We sure spend a lot of time looking though! Money, power, sex, drugs, and of course a great golf game are a few of the illusions we chase to find that "experience" we all are looking for. We continue to seek, but do not find. When we allow ourselves to question our values, motivation, and intentions for doing things, if we are completely honest, we realize that we feel empty and afraid. We continue to seek and we

73

continue to be disappointed. Why? Because we are looking for love in all the wrong places!

The wonderful news is, God is in everything! Even in every green we see! The problem is we fail to see the truth, because we are looking through a veil that separates us from the truth. God is *only* love, and there is no duality in **Her**. *(Had to do it; this is a woman writing this book!)* *A Course in Miracles*, described as being a course in mind training, is asking us to choose to align our thoughts with the Holy Spirit within, rather than the ego. The Holy Spirit will undo the error of our thinking and lead us to clearer vision. Although in truth, we have no need for healing because all is already perfect, God realized that we have our roots firmly planted in the ego world, a.k.a. *"the dream."* She, "God," sent to us the Holy Spirit to meet us where we are. Do you want peace? The Holy Spirit will meet you exactly where you are and will lead you there. The clearer your vision becomes, you will see God in every green, every fairway, every shot, and every encounter of your life.

One of my favorite quotes from *A Course in Miracles* is: *"When you meet anyone, remember it is a holy encounter...for in him* (that person or encounter) *you will find yourself or lose yourself."* Choose the Holy Spirit, you will find God; choose the ego, you will find nothing! It's up to you.

Charlotte is perhaps the only person I know who could combine the concepts of money, power, sex, drugs, and *"a great golf game"* into the same sentence. *(I'm surprised she left out "rock and roll!")* But all kidding aside, the very valid point she is making is that with **all** of these illusions – and we could add high stakes poker, short track speed skating, French cuisine, scuba diving, bungee jumping, or anything else we wanted to add to that list – it is ultimately the *experience* we are seeking, and we are pursuing any of those goals or activities in hopes of finding that experience.

Of course, ultimately it is only the personal experience of our *true nature* – our completeness and Oneness in God – that can fulfill *all* of our desires fully and totally.

And here in Hole 10 of *A Golf Course in Miracles*, we get to see another example of what I like to think of as Char's ***"payback on Jesus,"*** as her form of wry compensation for his having dictated *A Course in Miracles* using symbolically "masculine" terminology! All of those references to *"brothers"* and *"Sons of God,"* and especially the repeated references to God as our *"Father"* were simply too much for my co-author, and the response was inevitable, obviously…

I am *kidding* once again, of course! My dear friend Charlotte knows, as well as anyone (and she teaches this as well), that in truth, God has no gender; God is *all* gender. Stated simply and accurately, ***God Is.*** But rather than get caught up in semantics, and especially since the Course is meant to be ultimately practical, it makes sense to phrase things in ways that most people can readily follow and understand. And being that masculine usage has been somewhat the norm in English language literature, as well as in most spiritual scripture (and this is not to say that that's a ***better*** way…it just is what it is), the Course was written using these forms of terminology as well.

It is widely understood by most figures in the Course community that if anyone has any kind of problem with the masculine nature of the words being used…then just change the words! Meaning, if "Sons of God" seems offensive, just read it for yourself as "Daughters of God," or "Children of…" or "Creation of…" The meaning of the message doesn't change, and that's all that really matters. When referring to our "brothers," just substitute "sisters" or even "siblings" (to be completely gender-neutral), if that helps the message come through more smoothly. For myself, rather than refer to God as "Himself" or "Herself," I often use the term *"Godself,"* as in, "God created us as an extension of Godself."

See? Clear and accurate, and blissfully gender-neutral! As long as the *meaning* remains unchanged, feel free to make these kinds of substitutions wherever you feel guided to do so. And if, as Char has suggested, you wish to picture God as a woman, perhaps even swinging a Big Bertha golf club over her head, well that's just fine with me. *(In fact, I really **like** that idea!)*

So at this point, we begin to understand more clearly that God is in everything because *"God Is,"* and everything that is real is a creation and extension of God. That includes all of us, the "Creation of God," in our true state: perfect, invulnerable, and gender-free. And every form of peace, joy, and love that we can ever experience, all of this is of God, because all of this *is* God.

But what about the "illusion" we have been discussing? All of these things and thoughts that aren't really there? How can God be in every green I see, when the green isn't even actually real?

Come with me, my spiritual siblings, and let's ride in *God's Golf Cart* (a *pink* one, no doubt) and cruise on over to Hole 11 for some answers!

Hole 11

"God is in every green I see because God is in my golf bag."

(Inspired by A Course in Miracles: Workbook *Lesson 30)*

"God is in everything I see because God is in my mind."

If you have taken the previous lessons into consideration, you are most likely starting to see and experience things different than you did before. In Hole 10, "God is in every green I see," you were introduced to the idea that God is everywhere. If in the past, you were not able to experience this idea, my hope is that you are having a few shifts in perception, *a.k.a.* the "miracle!"

Because God is in everything you see, that means that God is also in your golf bag. She is in every club, tee, ball, and glove. Pretty amazing to think about, isn't it? Very comforting and extremely powerful! You can never escape this truth. You, however, can choose not to invite Her into your round and your golf bag. You have been given the gift of free will. Each moment you are choosing to be powerful or powerless, peaceful or strained. Your experience is based solely upon the choices you make in each moment. Every stroke you make, every tee, fairway, green, sand trap and pond, God is there! What a gift, and yet you choose against this truth. You continue to play the game of golf and live life with such a limited perspective. Why? Because although you are not really thrilled with what you have made, it is familiar, and familiarity, although not so great, is comfortable. It is time to get out of your comfort zone! When you get out of the comfort zone, you are in the "God Zone!"

When you see a dancer, athlete, or anyone who is mastering their skill, it is a thing of beauty. There is no struggle or fear, but rather a dance with the universe. When a man or woman is performing at a high level, they are oblivious to what is going on around them; they are fully present. You too have this potential, because God is in your golf bag!

In each of the *Holes* (or chapters) here in *A Golf Course in Miracles*, we are adapting teachings from *A Course in Miracles* and presenting them in humorous ways, obviously – but also in ways that will actually serve to improve one's golf game, as well as, hopefully, one's overall experience of life in general. At the same time, though, we always want to recognize and facilitate a deeper understanding of the broader teachings of the Course itself, which can eventually help us attain a state where our Earthly concerns will no longer seem so concerning to us.

ACIM Lesson 30 states, ***"God is in everything I see because God is in my mind."*** The lesson tells us, *"The idea for today is the spring-board for vision. From this idea will the world open up before you, and you will look upon it and see in it what you have never seen before."* It goes on to instruct us about recognizing this new kind of vision, in which *"we are trying to see in the world what is in our minds, and what we want to recognize is there. Thus, we are trying to join with what we see, rather than keeping it apart from us."*

What we see in the world is what is in our minds, what is our ***projection***. And if God is in our minds, then we can see that which we choose to "think with God," rather than the illusory projections of the ego. So even though God is not "in" the illusory, unreal world, God can be (and is) in the vision we choose to see with, when we choose to think and see with God, and not with the ego.

Deep stuff once again, yes, I know…but here's the basic point: God is not "in" anything within the illusion (and in that sense, God cannot actually be "in" every green I see), yet God *is* in my mind; to be completely accurate, God *is* my mind, my *real* mind. Therefore, when I am choosing to think and see "with God," any vision that I seem to behold will actually contain the essence and reflection of God's truth in it.

So what's this business about God being in my golf bag? *(Can't a guy or gal get any privacy anywhere?)* Actually, the whole idea of privacy is rather meaningless as far as God is concerned – but that's another topic entirely! Here's the golf bag concept. Your golf bag is essentially a very elaborate and well-equipped toolkit. It holds all the "stuff" you need for a game of golf: your clubs, golf balls, tees, gloves, snacks and liquid sustenance, perhaps an umbrella, maybe a good-luck charm with Ben Hogan's picture on it. All your "tools of the trade," everything you need to give the game your best shot(s).

Now if God is in your mind, and hence, in everything you see… then God is (in that sense) in your golf bag as well! God is in every club you swing, each ball you play with…God is in *you*. And in that knowledge, you can do no wrong! And if a shot "appears" to go badly, you can react to that *as you choose to,* and experience all the joy and peace that you choose to experience, without any part of what's "not real" intruding upon your inner peace – or your *"inner par"* – as long as you know that God is in your mind, and is in every green you see, because God is always right there with you, *in* you – and in your golf bag!

Hole 12

"I am not the victim of the hole I bogey."

(Inspired by A Course in Miracles: Workbook *Lesson 31)*

"I am not the victim of the world I see."

There are so many circumstances in our lives and the lives of others where we see ourselves as victims. The economy, world affairs, crime, illness, and relationships are only a few areas in our life experience where we allow ourselves to justify our reasoning for being a victim. What about the victims of a natural disaster or an accident? Of course, who in their right mind would not see them as victims? But I want to ask you a question: What is being in your right mind, and what *is* a victim?

Being a victim is a great tool for the ego to keep us stuck in our littleness. The news, magazines, television, and newspapers all sustain themselves by reinforcing all of the drama in the world. We watch, read and discuss the latest news and respond by saying, "Ain't it awful," or, "the world is going to hell in a hand basket!" When we see these things, of course we *are* affected. We have empathy, we have compassion; but we are not victims!

A Course in Miracles comes from a perspective of "black and white," "love or fear," leaving no room for that "gray area." Although a very difficult concept at first, with practice and vigilance, we begin to see and experience the world through a different prism. This new paradigm or vision enables us to see beyond the form, and experience the formless.

The Course demands of us a level of spiritual maturity that requires us to understand that we are 100 percent responsible for the world we see! Although to many, that idea is threatening and ridiculous, it is actually the most empowering thing you can do for yourself. If you are not a victim and you are 100 percent responsible for what you see, you can change it! How empowering is that? Give yourself a moment to think about that one. OK, minute's up. How does it feel to know that although you have experienced things that were not so great in the past, you can release the past, be present in this moment, and co-create your future with the Holy Spirit!

What about those bogeys? You are not a victim of those either! Even if you hit the most perfect shot to the green, and a dog comes up and takes off with your golf ball, you are not a victim. You are playing a match; you are two up with three holes to go. All of a sudden, your opponent's ball hits your arm and you cannot swing the club and you lose the match. Are you a victim then? Only if you want to be!

Life will always present bogeys, sand traps, and water hazards. But you no longer need to be a victim of them. How you respond to the "hazards" of life is what makes you great. When you are experiencing bogeys, sand traps, or a golf ball-stealing dog, take a deep breath, say to yourself, "I can see pars and birdies instead of this," and allow yourself to be responsible for all things. This shift in perception, a.k.a. the "miracle," enables you to shift from victim to victor, from bogeys to birdies, from powerless to powerful.

Just like going to the gym, the more you go, the better your results. The same holds true with training your mind. The more you choose to shift your perception from bogeys to birdies, the more you will reap the rewards as well. The reward is inner-peace, a.k.a. *inner-par!*

This is another one of those concepts that can be addressed at two levels: the deeper, more meaningful level which *A Course in Miracles* addresses, and the more Earthly level of *"the golf course,"* the level which we are learning is not actually real (but as long as it's the world we still *seem* to be living and interacting in, we address it as well).

At the deeper metaphysical level, the reason the Course teaches that *"I am not the victim of the world I see"* is because if I am responsible for everything I seem to see and experience, if I am in fact actually projecting all that I think I see, then how can I possibly be the victim of it? Now once again, when we say *"I"* am responsible, and *"I"* am projecting, we don't mean me and you or any other individual as the physical human beings we appear to be. We are referring to that level of our existence of which we, at least in general, are not consciously aware; it is from that state that we are responsible for projecting all of this world that we seem to perceive.

Now there we've gone and gotten all deep again. But one of the things we've learned is that the metaphysics taught by *A Course in Miracles* is really ***"spirituality for grown-ups!"*** The truth isn't sugarcoated and made artificially easier to swallow, presented as a fairy tale for children, and for those who don't want to have to examine things too deeply. But if you are essentially stuck in a dream and you want to wake up, you're not going to accomplish that by choosing what is simply a different dream…you're going to have to choose *reality* instead of *any* dream.

None of this means, however, that you can't enjoy parts of the dream while you still seem to be dreaming! As long as you keep your "eye on the ball" (in this case, *The Holy Spirit's Golf Ball of Enlightenment™*) – meaning that you continue focusing on developing your awareness of simply being the *observer* of what seems to be happening here – you can certainly continue to enjoy the happier aspects of the illusion, even while you're ultimately learning to eventually leave all illusion behind.

So how do we apply this principle to our *Golf Course in Miracles* concept of *"I am not the victim of the hole I bogey"?* It's not really so difficult, when we dismiss the idea of victimhood entirely! How can any of us be a victim of something that was our own idea? And what if we could take whatever seemed to happen to us, and see it as a source of humor, and perhaps even as an experience that we could benefit from?

What if, as in Charlotte's terrific example of a stray dog running off with our golf ball, we chose to see it instead as something hysterically funny, like a scene from a comedy movie! *(Hmmm…now that I think about it, wasn't there actually a scene like that in the movie Caddyshack? Wait; that might have been a gopher…)*

Or perhaps you're about to make your first hole-in-one: perfect shot, the ball is rolling straight at the pin, and right at the last moment, an errant blade of grass pops up and deflects your ball away from dropping into the hole. *"Aarrghh!"* A victim? Or have you perhaps been granted a tremendous **gift**—the unique ability to now see the illusory universe as completely absurd and ridiculously impossible, something that without question must have been made up, as nothing this perverse could possibly happen naturally in any sane version of reality!

You can't be a victim if you choose to see everything as being presented for your own benefit and amusement, can you? So with that understanding, it's easy to see that you can't possibly be the victim of the hole you bogey!

Hole 13

"There is another way of looking at this wood."

(Inspired by A Course in Miracles: Workbook *Lesson 33)*

"There is another way of looking at the world."

Every moment of every day, we are being bombarded with images, stories and heated talks in the clubhouse about politics, the wars, the economy, and suffering in the world. Many of us choose our favorite news channels, magazines, and peers that support our views of how we perceive the world. Some of us spend many hours in a day listening to and sharing our opinions of the current state of affairs. This is how we see the world. We are seeing the world by our dominant thoughts, opinions, and ideas of others. Once we have established our viewpoint and found a support system to reinforce it, we have quite a ball of energy created around these beliefs. What great stories we all have made up! These "stories" seem to be our reality. Is this, your current reality, really all that you want in your life?

As we explored earlier, the universe is pure energy. Our thoughts projected upon this energy are constantly creating our experience. Literally, *"change your thoughts, change your life!"* There is another way of looking at this world: through the eyes and vision of love. Love is a choice that we must make to see the world as it truly is: perfect. *"Seek not to change the world, but rather change your mind about the world."*

*"There is another way of looking at this **wood**!"* For those of you that have not played golf for more than twenty years, you may not have any idea what this statement means! Believe it or not, before there were *"Big Berthas,"* woods at one time were actually made of wood! I was given my first "metal wood" in 1978, and was fascinated by the concept. A metal wood, how will that work? I came from using real "wood woods" made out of persimmon or laminated wood. They were so beautiful! Polished and shiny in a variety of colors (the more traditional players held true to black, blond, or brown), but I can still remember my turquoise laminated "Ben Hogan" woods, and later I manifested my custom persimmon wood clubs in a deep red; they were beautiful!

It took me a while to make the complete break from wood to metal. I still remember showing up at the 1988 U.S. Women's Open with my woods and my blades! You can bet after I got back home I made the shift to the latest that technology had to offer!

It also can take us a while to make the break from illusion to reality in our minds. It was ten years before I could let go of my attachment to my nostalgic equipment. After resisting, I realized there were options for me to play better and with more ease. The same holds true in consciousness. At first, your view of the world seems to make sense, you have attracted exactly what you need to support your beliefs and you will defend your beliefs to anyone who challenges them.

So often, our stories are made up out of judgment, anger, and old paradigms. These programs are rooted deeply in our subconscious minds. All of our stories are from the "past," and the past is over. When the past is brought into the present moment, there is no space for creation.

Ask yourself these questions. Am I happy? Am I peaceful? Do I see beauty in all things? Am I willing to forgive all thoughts that have hurt me? If you can answer yes to all of the above questions, I honor you. You are free of both the good and not so good opinions of others! And yet, if your desire is to be better, and do better, you can.

There is another way to see this world. You can see this world in its perfection and beauty. There is only one thing you have to do: *Forgive!* Forgiveness means that I am willing to surrender my limited vision and ask to see the world through the vision of love. *Ask, and you will receive.* It is so easy to get clouded vision by our judgments. It is also easy to make another choice. Choosing new vision will enable you to experience a world far greater than anything this world has to offer. Just as I found another way of looking at my woods, you can find another way of looking at the world!

I don't lay claim to being much of a high-quality golfer. In fact, I plan to have my lovely and talented co-author give me some formal lessons, so I can finally learn to play the game properly! Back when I was in college *(many years ago, I admit!)*, I actually took a phys-ed class in golf, believe it or not. Unfortunately, though, I think that class probably did me more harm than good!

*(Unlike Charlotte's enlightened style of Zen golf instruction, my college golf teacher back then tried to **totally** change every aspect of the way I naturally played golf...and in the process, completely eliminated whatever intuitive talent I may have already had at that time. It's a long story...)*

But before I ever played golf, I played guitar. Electric guitars back in the 1960s used amplifiers with vacuum tubes *(also referred to as "valves", particularly in the U.K.)* to generate sound; this was before transistors began to take over, and long before digital audio had even been heard of. Tube amps were heavy (and generated lots of heat), and the tubes inside were fragile and subject to breaking... but they sounded wonderful!

As time went on, by the late 1960s and early 70s, solid-state transistor driven equipment was taking over. The amps were more powerful (and undoubtedly cheaper to manufacture), and many players were making the switch, with old-style tube amps becoming harder to find. Who would want to use that old-fashioned tube technology, anyway, when all these *modern* amps were available?

But over time, people began to realize that those new-fangled amplifiers just didn't sound as good as the old ones! It turns out that the older vacuum tube technology, for all its inherent limitations, actually added something to the sonic picture that could just make electric guitars sound **great**. And so, many players started going back to, and demanding, the older style tube amps. Today, the more expensive and desirable guitar amps are tube/valve designs, and older vintage amps from the 50s and 60s are the most highly prized and sought after.

So, what happened...did tubes change, and suddenly start sounding better than they had before? No, of course not. Guitar players just started looking at tubes and amplifiers in a different way, not just as a means to make an electric guitar *louder*, but as a *tone-shaping device*, to make the guitar sound *better* than it could have sounded without that tube-driven amp working alongside it.

"There is another way of looking at that amp."

"There is another way of looking at this wood."

"There is another way of looking at the world."

There is another way of looking at **everything**...both in terms of changing our opinion about it, and choosing to see it in a different light, but also in the deeper sense, and in the manner that Charlotte mentioned—seeing it through the vision of Love.

Golf technology has followed a different path than guitar amplifier technology. It is not likely that golfers will suddenly discover that older clubs actually work better than the newer ones! As Charlotte has described, modern materials and designs have made today's golf clubs perform far better than the clubs of the past.

But the principle remains the same. However we think we see anything at the moment, we must remember that there is another way of looking at it. Whether it is golfing technology, musical technology, or **anything** that we appear to see in the material world, we can either see it through the eyes of judgment, or through the loving sight forgiveness brings.

Judgment always involves the past. And as we have been discussing in this book, the past does not actually exist! In reality, it is always **"now,"** and the past is just a thought (and merely one of those *illusory* thoughts, at that.) So to judge anything is, ultimately, to see it only as a part of the past, and not to experience it the way we could by looking at it in another way...and right now.

The only concept of judgment that can have **any** reality and true value must be the judgment that comes from the Holy Spirit, from

91

God's vantage point...from that highest of perspectives where *ALL* is known in complete and total accuracy and understanding, and without any of the built-in limitations that are unavoidable from our human perspective.

There is a section in *A Course in Miracles* (in Part Two of the Workbook, from *Instruction 10)* titled *"What is the Last Judgment?"* which tells us: *"The final judgment on the world contains no condemnation. For it sees the world as totally forgiven... You who believed that God's Last Judgment would condemn the world to hell along with you, accept this holy truth: God's Judgment is the gift of the Correction He bestowed on all your errors, freeing you from them, and all effects they ever seemed to have. To fear God's saving grace is but to fear complete release from suffering, return to peace, security and happiness, and union with your own Identity."*

"Your own Identity." This is the level where we truly exist, as we truly are. No longer in the world of illusion, in the forms of these seemingly separated beings, but as the perfect creation that is our Reality. We no longer require nor even desire any concept of judgment, as complete forgiveness has released us from any belief in the past, or even the vaguest perception of anything that is part of any illusory world.

Forgiveness is a "letting go," a total release of anything that does not really exist. It is literally the opposite of judgment, which is a "holding on" to the past—to grievances, to anger, even to subconscious beliefs, and the idea that anything in this physical world could actually be real. Forgiveness *releases*, here in the eternal "now," what judgment would imprison in the past.

So when looking at anything in the world, remember to say, *"Goodbye, past!"* and choose again to see it in the present moment, free of all limiting judgments and past beliefs. Treat yourself to the *freedom* of seeing whatever seems to be in front of you cleanly, clearly, peacefully, and joyfully, without preconceived notions of any kind.

And the next time you're about to hit your first drive off that tee, as you look down at your perfect grip on the club in your hands, remember to tell yourself very happily, ***"There is another way of looking at this wood!"***

Hole 14

"God plays with me wherever I go."

(Inspired by A Course in Miracles: Workbook *Lesson 41)*

"God goes with me wherever I go."

As golfers, we love a change in scenery, a new challenge. It is always fun and exciting to experience new courses. We love to put our game to the test on as many different golf courses as we can. That is what makes golf unique as compared to any other sport. Tennis courts look the same, baseball fields look the same, basketball courts and hockey fields look the same, and all bowling alleys are bound by the same dimensions as well.

Every golf course has its own personality. Based on the geography, the terrain can vary greatly. Mountains, oceans, rolling hills, and the desert all lend themselves to a design appropriate to its surroundings. We plan our vacations around golf; we make friends with the guy who is the member at the club that we can't wait to play. Not only is every course different, no round of golf is the same twice on any course. The weather, pin and tee placements, and change of seasons will make every round of golf a new adventure.

Isn't it nice to know that "God plays with you wherever you go!" From Pebble Beach to St. Andrews, and everywhere in between, God is there! *Good* is there! Your "inner teacher" is there, waiting to be asked what to do next. And yet, so often we rely on the past – not because it worked so well before, but because it is familiar. God is in every green, every ball, every tee, in your golf bag, and in your mind, and yet you feel alone. So whether you are playing at your home course or a thousand miles away, remember: "God plays with you wherever you go!"

Yes, isn't it nice to know that wherever you go, whatever course you may be playing on, and at any time of day, night, or season...your best golf instructor, caddie, coach, and peak performance analyst is right there with you? You are never alone, trying to make decisions (and the shots and strokes that result from them) without having the best expert guidance and support just a simple thought away!

God plays with you wherever you go, because God goes with you wherever you go. God created us as an extension of Godself. (And since time is part of the *"illusion,"* and it is really always *"now,"* we are actually always in a continuous state of creation by God.) So, as the extension of God, we are never apart from God, and we can never be separated from our Source. Therefore, in the truest sense, we are never alone.

Speaking of my own experience, I can honestly say that I no longer ever feel entirely alone. Having studied these principles and having put this thought system into practice for a good many years now, I have come to *know* beyond any doubt that I am always connected to my Source, that I am not separated and alone, and that wherever I may seem to go, the power and the presence that created me is always there with me—my active partner and companion in everything I think, see, and do.

I am far from perfect *(just ask Charlotte...or my lovely wife, Helen!)* And I have certainly not reached the state of perfect enlightenment. (Not *yet*, anyway!) But one of the nicest things about the kind of spiritual development that we are discussing here is the fact that it is a *cumulative* process; one does not have to "master it all" before seeing results. Each little bit we learn, each concept we come to accept and understand, each element of the process we undertake, brings its own immediate rewards, even while we build toward still greater results as we progress further.

So at every stage of our development, we *experience* the changes that are taking place. And *experience*, rather than just an intellectual understanding of principles, is what turns a belief into a *knowing*—a certainty of Truth that can never falter nor fail, no matter what worldly circumstances appear to take place. And the actual experience of God, the *"knowing beyond any doubt"* that we are at all times linked to our Creator, sustainer, provider, and protector, results in a condition of knowing—*really experiencing!*—that we are never lonely, never alone, and never abandoned.

The ego thrives on the feeling (deep down inside all of us at one time or another) that we are ultimately "separate" and alone, hiding inside our own little "cave" of isolation, fearfully looking out onto a dangerous world. And in Earthly terms, the world does indeed seem fearful! The cave-dwelling world of our ancestors was undoubtedly far more dangerous than even our present world appears to be. *Remember, the ego has been at this game for a long, long time!* And

97

we maintain the remnants of the many millennia of those fear-based thoughts and images deep within the hard-wiring of our collective neurology and consciousness.

But our salvation from this seemingly endless cycle of fear lies in the very experience of *Oneness* that we are describing, the unmistakable recognition of the presence of God, there with us at all times and in all places. So wherever we may appear to be, and whether we are swinging our club as a golfer or as a caveman *(or cavewoman, as well),* we can always know beyond any question, that *"God plays with me wherever I go!"*

Hole 15

"My hooks are images that I have made."

(Inspired by A Course in Miracles: Workbook *Lesson 15)*

"My thoughts are images that I have made."

Scientific research has been working on and is coming closer to finding the meaning of God. The pursuit of this discovery has been explored by scholars, theologians, and lay people, who have yet to find a conclusive answer/meaning to *what* and *who* God is.

The introduction to *A Course in Miracles* states:

"This is a course in miracles. It is a required course. Only the time you take it is voluntary. Free will does not mean that you can establish the curriculum. It means only that you can elect

what you want to take at a given time. **The course does not aim at teaching the meaning of love, for that is beyond what can be taught. It does aim, however, at removing the blocks to the awareness of love's presence, which is your natural inheritance.** *The opposite of love is fear, but what is all-encompassing can have no opposite."*

We call Earth our home amidst a forever-expanding universe of infinite beauty and possibility. There are theories in science – and they are supported by *A Course in Miracles* – that we have made the entire universe up! Wow! What a concept…and what an idea to wrap our minds around!

Our thoughts are things. Our thoughts infused with emotion and projected upon universal energy are continually creating images. We have literally made this entire dream up! Within you is the power to choose and to create images based on fear, or images based on love. Each of us has free will to choose which direction to follow. When we choose to align our thoughts and feelings to love, we are choosing to co-create with the mind of infinite possibility.

Our desire then, becomes that of joining rather than separation. Allowing the infinite mind to be our guide, allows us to be fully in the present moment, free of any past memories or images in our minds. When we plug our thoughts into the fear based, or ego mind, we are making a decision to pull from past images and programs that which is familiar and comfortable. When we choose to live our lives by acting on that which is comfortable and familiar we are stifling our spiritual and emotional growth and not making a space for our creativity to come forth.

By now, I hope you are recognizing that to live in mastery, you must release the past. These programs, although deeply rooted in your subconscious mind, can be changed through practice. To be in good physical condition, you exercise regularly, watch your diet, and you then see the results—a.k.a. *Cause and Effect.* Just like exercise and diet produce a healthy body, and hitting balls on the range with a conscious purpose improves your ball striking ability, the same holds true for spiritual practice.

If you *really* wanted peace, you would have it. The truth is, most of us don't want to let go of certain personality traits or attachments. To be at peace and to be enlightened calls for rigorous honesty. You have to be willing to look at, *and* question every value you hold. How many times in a day do you choose against peace? How often do you exempt someone from your heart? How many grievances are you holding on to? Peace is yours for the asking, but not without a price. The price is letting go of the past, being willing to forgive, and choosing love!

"My hooks are images that I have made."

Example: you have an approach to a green. It is 150 yards away. You choose the appropriate club, look at the flag and where you want the ball to go. You then step up to the ball and take a swing. Rather than hitting a nice little draw or fade to the flag, you manage to hit the ugliest hook you have ever hit. It goes directly into the woods, just where you did not want to go!

The club may get slammed to the ground, a few choice words may come out—you are ticked! Obviously, you did not intend to hit a hook. You envisioned a perfect shot, landing on the green, rolling to the pin with a tap-in for birdie. Now you will be lucky to escape with a bogey!

I invite you again, to re-consider this; **you are 100 percent responsible for the world you see.** Does that mean that you chose the hook? In truth, yes. But most likely, not on a conscious level. The "image" of a hook is somewhere in your mind and in your body. Although you had other plans, the hook decided to come out and play. Think of an iceberg in the middle of the ocean. You may only see 10 percent of it above the surface of the water. What lies beneath the water is the other

90 percent. The iceberg is a metaphor for your subconscious mind. Although you don't see it, it is there, just like the iceberg. I recently heard a statement that our subconscious mind is **one million** times more powerful than our conscious mind! Although that may be an over statement, it sure got my attention! Knowledge is power. Rather than feel overwhelmed and hopeless at the dominance of our subconscious mind, take action...reprogram it!

Now that you are accepting responsibility for your experience on the golf course, you are also claiming the ability and power to change it! Very good news! First, cause is thought. Are your thoughts in alignment with that which you are choosing to create? If so, become emotionally involved with that thought. Visualize as clear an image as you can and hold onto it. You can now take action based on that image. Action may include an adjustment in your swing or grip, spending more time on the range to develop muscle memory in your body for the desired outcome of your shots. A simple question to ask yourself is, "Will this thought or action move me in the direction of my goal?" If so, do it! If not, choose again.

Your hooks will become a thing of the past, and your game is yours for creating!

If a hook is a mistake, then it cannot be real. Let's face it, if the ball itself is not actually real, and the club in my hand and the fairway out in front of me are equally unreal, then the image of the accursed golf ball curving far off track from my desired path for it cannot be real either. So what is it that I seem to be seeing?

What I think I am seeing is actually an image that I have made. I have made this image both within my visual apparatus – my eyes, brain, the related parts of the body that appear to exist within the physical, illusory universe – but also, and more importantly (as well as more accurately), I have made this image within my mind. As Charlotte has stated, *"First, cause is thought."* First, we have the thought about the image; *then*, we seem to see the image itself. It also matters not if the image appears to take place outside of us, or simply within our mind itself. Either way, the apparent reality of it is the same in our perception.

This is why the whole concept of "visualization" has any merit at all. When we actively create the experience of an image within our consciousness, our human mind (and even our physical neurology) treats it *as if it were entirely real*...yielding positive *or negative* results for us, depending on what it is we have projected and chosen to experience in this manner.

So yes, we can repeatedly envision the image of our making the "perfect swing" (or the perfect example of any action we might wish to undertake), and it has been proven that our performance abilities in that area will indeed improve, even though our participation in this exercise has only been "in our mind." As far as our conscious-ness is concerned, that part doesn't matter.

But the opposite of this scenario has just as powerful an effect on us, as well. When we create the image of something we *don't* want – a hook, a slice, a missed tennis shot, a poorly played musical note, a bad performance at work – *whatever* it might be, that "negative image" will be viewed with just as much perceived reality by our human consciousness as the "preferred" images would have been... with the results and effects of *those* images becoming just as "real" in our human experience.

A Course in Miracles teaches us, **"My thoughts are images that I have made."** And the word "image" does not only refer to a visual picture; one definition of the word *image* is *"an iconic mental repre-sentation."* Therefore, every thought we have is an image, a mental

103

representation of some concept in our awareness. The Course is telling us that these thoughts are images that we have made; it is not as if they existed previously, and only now are we aware of them...*we made them,* and that is why we think we see them.

All of this of course directly relates to the *Course in Miracles* concept that *"My mind holds only what I think with God,"* as well as our *Golf Course in Miracles* idea that *"My drive holds only what I swing with God."* Both of these teachings differentiate between our illusory, ego-based thoughts (and the images that we made) and our *real* thoughts—the thoughts we think with God.

But here in our apparent reality, in the material-world situations with which we seem to be dealing, we find very practical applications of these concepts as well. If my thoughts, and my **hooks** – or any problematic outcomes I may encounter – are really presenting themselves as the results and effects of images that I have made... then I can change those images, and thereby change those results and effects! I can begin, right now (*now* being the only time there actually is) to make new images. The old images that I seem to have made previously, images of failure and frustrations, of hooks, slices, and the endless variety of screw-ups that life seems to invariably present us with, can be replaced by new images that I have made *now:* images of whatever I want to see, and choose to experience.

Even though this material universe isn't actually real, we still feel as if we are here in it, at least for a while yet. Yes, we are hopefully (and continually) moving toward that awareness of pure *Oneness* that will transcend and replace all illusion, and any thought or image of failure and frustration of any kind – on the golf course, in the sports arena, in the workplace, or in our personal relationships. And when we reach that state, we are not going to care one little bit about any of the illusory images we might ever have made, back when we believed we were caught up in an ongoing dream of separation. We won't even choose to remember that we mistakenly thought we **had** this crazy dream!

But for the moment, as long as we still seem to have some vested interest in seeing this dream-process through, why not make our shared illusion a more peaceful and joy-filled one? We can change those thoughts, those images, those hooks, and any other experiences we seem to be having…and we can make those changes right *now!*

Hole 16

"I have no neutral stance;
I see no neutral grip."

(Inspired by A Course in Miracles: Workbook *Lessons 16/17)*

"I have no neutral thoughts. I see no neutral things."

I have been a seeker of spiritual truth for the better part of my life, all in a quest to discover the "holy grail," the "secrets of the universe!" Being born into a practicing protestant family, my early roots were grounded in Christianity. My experiences in the Methodist church were only positive. Our ministers and Sunday school teachers presented their teachings in a lovable and practical way and enabled me to perceive God as a loving being. Although my experience in church was only good, my soul was yearning to learn more. In my late teens, I began a spiritual journey that I am still on today.

I have spent time getting to know the world's major religions and philosophies in a *Readers Digest* version. My goal is to find that which is the common thread that weaves all of the great religions and philosophies together. I set my intention to find a teaching that would answer my request for truth, and my life was transformed when I was introduced to *A Course in Miracles.*

Instead of bar hopping, I was a church and new age bookstore hopper! One evening while browsing the books in a bookstore in West Palm Beach, Florida, a woman from out of the blue said to me, "You must read this!" The book she was sharing with me was *A Course in Miracles*! She was so excited and enthusiastic. I felt compelled to buy it, and I did! Once I got home with my latest book purchases, I flipped through the pages and noticed the book read more like a textbook than my usual easy readers that I usually chose. The book ended up on the shelf, not to be opened again...*Yet!*

As a golf teaching professional, I had the pleasure of teaching in Florida in the winter and New York in the summer. In New York, I taught at a beautiful club in Scarsdale: Quaker Ridge. To this day, it is one of the greatest golf courses I have ever played. The club provided housing and I had a private room that overlooked the golf course. The accommodations were simple but nice, but if I wanted a television, I would have to bring it. I chose not to bring a TV, but rather bring the box of my unread books and spend some time reading them.

One of the books in the box was, *you guessed it, A Course in Miracles*. I remember reading the introduction to it and a sense of peace came over me. I felt like I was home. I continued to read further, but I found the content difficult to understand. The book went back into the box, but it was not forgotten...

When I began reading the Course again, I immediately felt a sense of peace and connection to spirit. Its words immersed my soul and I knew it was the path for me!

It became my mission to learn more about this course, *and I did!* I eventually found study groups in Florida and made it my business to learn all that I could about the Course and its teachings!

Neutral stance? Neutral grip? Neutral thoughts and things? Where does this fit into the prior paragraphs? In my quest, I have discovered for myself that if I were to describe God/Love in one word, it would be "neutral." In our Judeo-Christian model of God, we are taught that He/She is vengeful, and a force to be reckoned with. A vengeful God was not what my experience had been, but along the way, there have been many people whom I have met who were not so lucky.

The Course and its teachings reinforced the belief that I already had, that God is unconditional with His/Her love and has never judged us! It goes on to explain that we don't need to ask for forgiveness, because we have never been judged!

I will address the next question that is most likely on your mind; "If there is only neutrality, and there is no judgment, then everyone in the world would just go crazy!" Actually, the contrary is true. The Course teaches us that although neutrality is the goal, we have lots of atoning to do before we can experience it. "Atoning," or the "undoing of fear," occurs when we allow the Holy Spirit or our higher self to guide us in all of our encounters.

There is an exercise in the Course *(in Lesson 71)* that states:

What would You have me do?
Where would You have me go?
What would You have me say, and to whom?

By following these instructions, you will only make decisions based on love and joining. The Holy Spirit within you will remove the blocks to the awareness of love's presence and you will become more neutral. Your super highs and your super lows will become

109

more stable. You will gain emotional control and you will not be dependent on external circumstances to experience peace. You will discover that peace and love already exist within you.

Back to how this relates to your stance and grip – *it really doesn't, much*, but it rather makes a point that has been made many times already. When you are in the past, you cannot be neutral. Release the past, practice following the voice of truth, and you will begin to experience neutrality or peace with your stance, grip, and every aspect of your game!

* Just a little tip on the grip: If your grip is too neutral, you will probably have a hard time generating much power and you may fight a slice! A stronger grip (position, not pressure) will produce stronger shots!

The "neutral" aspect of one's stance or grip, as far as golf is concerned, refers to a completely neutral position where the player is in his or her most basic, natural form, neither influencing the flight of the ball in one direction nor another, but simply allowing it to attain its movement in the most natural and straightforward way possible.

Now, as Charlotte has instructed in her golf tip on this subject, in practicality, one does not want to use a grip that is **too** neutral, or not enough power will be generated in the swing. We still, after all, are playing the game, and have to exert *some* influence over the path and flight of the ball! So a "happy medium" is what we are shooting for in the game of golf. Perhaps in this case, it's actually *good* that we have no neutral stance, or see a neutral grip!

But in the bigger picture, *A Course in Miracles* teaches us that, *"I have no neutral thoughts,"* and, *"I see no neutral things."* Those two phrases refer to the same thing, really, as we have already been taught that *"My thoughts are images that I have made."* So the things (images) we seem to see are actually our thoughts, anyway. But why are these things and thoughts not ever neutral?

The answer lies in the fact that *all* of this, every thought we have, every image we make, everything we see…all of it, *every part of it,* has *some* effect on us, and on what we believe. *Nothing is neutral!* There is not one thought we have but does not have an effect of some kind and some magnitude upon our belief system. In fact, we could say that it is the accumulation of all of these thoughts and "things" that is the *cause* of our belief system, and is in fact the cause of the illusory universe itself.

A Course in Miracles deals with this idea very directly, and several quotes from Workbook Lesson 16 *("I have no neutral thoughts")* give us unparalleled insight.

"There is no more self-contradictory concept than that of 'idle thoughts.' What gives rise to the perception of a whole world can hardly be called idle. Every thought you have contributes to truth or to illusion; either it extends the truth or it multiplies illusions."

Giving rise to the perception of an entire world, a vast universe… this is hardly the result of some inconsequential, *neutral* thing!

The Course's Lesson also teaches us to *"recognize that every thought you have brings either peace or war; either love or fear. A neutral result is impossible because a neutral thought is impossible. There is such a temptation to dismiss fear thoughts as unimportant, trivial and not worth bothering about that it is essential you recognize them all as equally destructive, but equally unreal."*

111

So all of those "little" negative thoughts, the ones we have become so used to easily dismissing as "too little to be concerned about," turn out to have been a force to be reckoned with all along, we now learn. All those little "fear thoughts" that flit across our minds with such regularity – the little worries and trepidations about our physical health, our relationships, our financial well-being, our golf game or tennis game, our prowess on the basketball court or in the boardroom *(or in the bedroom)*, our competitive ability to run a certain distance in a certain period of time – all of these "little" fear thoughts contribute to the picture of the world that we hold in our minds to be true. And part of the ego's game is to convince us that these "little" thoughts do not matter very much at all…just so that we will be nice and cooperative, and continue thinking them!

So how do we change our thinking in this area? *A Course in Miracles* gives us that answer in the same quote within which we are instructed in regard to fear thoughts: *"that it is essential you recognize them all as equally destructive, but equally unreal."*

"Equally unreal" is the key phrase. These fear thoughts are not our real thoughts, not the *thoughts we think with God,* as we discussed previously. God's thoughts, which we share in our true thinking, contain no elements of fear. *None!* Not only no *little* thoughts of fear and negativity, but absolutely none at all.

God's thoughts – therefore, our real thoughts – contain only the positive; and it is in this that we can align ourselves to alleviate the allegiance to fear that we have embraced up until now.

"Every thought you have contributes to truth or to illusion; either it extends the truth or it multiplies illusions." We can indeed contribute to the truth, and *extend* the truth, by choosing to align ourselves only with that pure expression of love and joy that is the essence of God's thinking and God's extension, without allowing the tiniest thought of the slightest cloud of fear to darken the Light.

It's a tall order, to be sure! But we can begin the process with some baby steps that will start us on our journey to the *"Land Where Fear Lives Not,"* every time we remember that whatever stance we take on the golf course or *anywhere* in our lives, and every time we "get a grip" on whatever challenge we are facing in any moment...in *all* of these situations, our thoughts about these things are **never** neutral. And every time we choose to not allow that tiniest of fear thoughts to even crop up in our minds, we are now one step closer to that *Heavenly Clubhouse* where "fear" is just a long-forgotten four-letter word!

Hole 17

"I seek but what score belongs to me in truth."

(Inspired by A Course in Miracles: Workbook *Lesson 104)*

"I seek but what belongs to me in truth."

The goal of most golfers is to shoot the best score they can. For some, that score may be even par, for others, 95 may be their target score. Whatever the score you are desiring to shoot, you most likely feel really, really good when you accomplish it, and not so good when you do not. The best way to chart your progress is to keep score, develop a handicap, and see where your game stands against par or the course rating.

Of course, score is an important factor of the game. If you play in leagues, compete with your buddies or play in tournaments, score is a factor. Score can also take the joy out of the game. I am a believer that golf is a game that is meant to be enjoyed. Whatever form that takes is different for everyone. For some, I suggest just to go out on the course, enjoy the surrounding beauty with people you like, and enjoy the day! Forget the scorecard! For others, keeping score is fun, and keeps things interesting. Keeping score allows you to see what direction your game is going.

Having been in the golf business for many years, I would see golfers stress over ladies' or men's day and stress out about who they were assigned to play with. If the pairing were desirable, they would be happy; if not, the golfers would be cranky and complain! Think of it as having two choices. When you get paired with someone that you perceive as ruining your round, you may decide that maybe ladies' or men's day is not for you. You may want to make your own game with people you like, and play by your own rules. Another option is to change your mind about that person you have allowed to ruin your game! Change your mind; change your experience. It works!

At country clubs, good news travels fast, and gossip travels even faster. Many times, before someone showed up for their first lesson, I had already heard the "dirt" on them. Betty is difficult! Bob is mean! Before each lesson, I would always ask the Holy Spirit to guide me so that I could provide the student with whatever it was they were meant to learn. If they were difficult, I saw that as a call for love, and I responded by giving love back rather than join their fear. I will tell you, I have given thousands of lessons over the years, and I can count on one hand how many students were difficult. You too, can make a decision to see a person in their truth, which is all good, or your pre-conceived idea of who they are, which is false!

"I seek what score belongs to me in truth," is about finding your "inner score," your place of contentment and peace on (and off) the course. So often, we are keeping score to the point it makes us uneasy and stressed. We want to see if we can get the most pars, the most money, the biggest house, or the most friends. All of these things are wonderful, but if you are ***needing*** these things or needing to have ***more*** in order to be happy or content, you will never find

116

peace. Seek what score belongs to you in truth! The essence of your being is already a "scratch" golfer!

Life *and* golf are meant to be enjoyed, and we each need to find our own way, not based on the good and not so good opinion of others. Keep score, have fun; don't keep score, have fun. Choose the one that fits you!

Our real message here in Hole 17 of *A Golf Course in Miracles* is not just about being truthful on your scorecard. It should pretty well go without saying that if your playing partners in a friendly round of golf find you cheating on your score, you may well find yourself tossed not so gently into a nearby water hazard! So plain old honesty, common sense, and fair play would all tell us that it's a good idea to be truthful and accurate in our score keeping.

Our message here runs a little deeper, and as we so often do in this book, we use golf as a metaphor for life in general. In this case, we can think of "score" as another word for "outcome," or "result," or whatever it is we are truly meant to have in any situation.

The Lesson from *A Course in Miracles*, upon which our message here is based, is simpler and more straightforward still: *"I seek but what belongs to me in truth."* *Whatever* it may be – score, outcome, result, anything at all – we are instructed to seek only that which belongs to us in truth. This is once again dealing with the concept of recognizing the difference between truth and illusion.

When we seek for "that which is not there," we are destined to be disappointed! If something does not really belong to us, if it is not our *"rightful inheritance,"* then it is certainly never going to make

117

us happy, or leave us feeling satisfied. This may seem like a very basic form of philosophy *(and I guess it is!)*, but it is worth a thorough examination. If we are seeking something that doesn't exist, or something that is *never* going to be rightfully ours, no matter what, how can we possibly expect to end up with a positive and satisfying result?

In very "Earthly" terms, this certainly makes sense. If our anticipated goal on the golf course is to shoot a perfect game every time out, we are definitely setting ourselves up for massive disappointment! If we are a musician looking for a *Number One* gold record with every song we write, or an investor seeking a gold-mine return on every investment he makes, once again, we would be living in dream land...and in those cases, it would not be *"happy dream"* land!

Now this doesn't mean that we should **not** set lofty goals and aspirations in life. *That's fine!* In this case, it is "attachment" to outcome that is the unrealistic – the *untruthful* – aspect involved. In our examples here, *"seeking but what belongs"* to us is the key principle – discovering what is really ours to have, focusing on that, and not being attached to an outcome that is in truth not meant to be ours in the first place.

But beyond this worldly level of concern there is a deeper meaning still, to this lesson. **"Seek"** is a powerful word; it is not indicating just something we are casually looking for, but something we are highly motivated to find. We are *"seeking"*...but seeking *what?*

We are seeking only that which belongs to us in truth; and what belongs to us in truth *is* the truth. We are not seeking illusions, or the unreal, or anything that will distract us from our true goal. Looking for a consistently perfect score on the golf course would imply that such a thing is even possible, and that it is somehow important for us to achieve. Seeking a massive return on every investment would imply that such a situation could actually occur, and that

118

somehow we *require* it, that we don't have enough already, that we are not "complete" without adding this improbable result to what we already have, in order to somehow make us feel "whole," and safe, and secure.

The truth about us is that we are already complete, and whole, and in an eternal state of perfect peace and endless joy. *We have just forgotten that for a time!* The good news is that we are now in the process of remembering it, of awakening to the truth about ourselves, and what it is we truly have. Learning to seek for **only** that which is ours *in truth* is a key step in our learning process.

We can still enjoy the games of the world, whether they are played out on golf courses, music stages, or the trading floor of the stock exchange. In fact, as we've said before, we can actually enjoy these pursuits **more** when we take them lightly, and detach ourselves from any expected outcomes! But as we learn the *truth about who and what we are,* and come to realize what we already have (and what we will **always** have, in truth), we will learn to **seek** only the real, only the truth...and let illusions be recognized for what they are: merely distractions, temporarily seeming to hold us back just a little while from attaining the goal that is truly ours to have.

Hole 18

"God's Will for me is perfect follow through."

(Inspired by A Course in Miracles: Workbook *Lesson 101)*

"God's will for me is perfect happiness."

A Course in Miracles teaches that the strangest belief that the ego has made is that our will and God's will are separate. We have based this belief on the idea that God's plan for us may not be what we want and so we continue to want to be in control. The ego's job is to keep us believing that God cannot possibly know what we *really* want, and that strange belief has us "shifting ceaselessly from one thing to another, still never finding what we want!" The truth is that God's will for us is perfect happiness – *and* a perfect follow-through!

Our will, and God's will cannot be separate. The spirit of God is within everyone, and that means **everyone!** Yes, even those actors on the stage of life who are playing a wonderful role as an "evil

121

doer!" The difference between *Mother Teresa* and let's say, *Bin Laden* for example, is that Mother Teresa chose to follow the voice of love within her. Bin Laden and other perceived "evil doers" followed the voice of fear, and that fear was based on programs of the past. But, beyond the roles each of us is playing, the essence of all of us is the same. When you perceive someone or a situation as being "dark" or "evil," rather than feed into the "sins" of another, ask for a miracle: make a decision to see the truth, the essence of the person or situation. The decision for peace rather than conflict will not only bring transformation to you, but will enable Spirit to bring forth greater meaning and understanding. A challenge, yes... but well worth the effort!

God's will for everyone is peace. God's will for everyone is Heaven. God's will for every golfer is a perfect follow-through if that is what they desire! We are the ones who limit our good, and we are the only ones who can make the decision to allow our good.

Your will and God's will are one in truth, for you are an extension of God's love and unlimited potential. It is impossible to be separate, but you have the choice whether or not you align with His/Her will or not. You have nothing to lose, and everything to gain!

Of the two authors of this book, I am the one who knows the least about golf. But even I know the importance of good follow-through to a golf swing! Just look at the swings of golfing greats such as Phil Mickelson, Annika Sorenstam, Tiger Woods, or Charlotte McGinnis *(OK, I admit I'm a little prejudiced in this area)*. But it is easy for anyone to see the grace, power, symmetry, and sheer beauty of those elegant golf swings.

So why is it even important what happens *after* the ball is struck? After the moment of impact, why is the rest of the swing of any concern at all? The answer lies in the fact that *all* of the elements of the swing – the back swing, the down swing, the actual striking of the ball, and the follow-through that comes after the impact – are "parts of the whole," and contribute to the subsequent flight of the golf ball…and the eventual outcome of the game.

It's very much like the psychological concept of *"gestalt,"* a German word that refers to something's "complete form" rather than just an isolated series of parts, and which recognizes a greater meaning and effectiveness based on that completeness. Seeing it this way, we realize that the follow-through is not simply an isolated action that happens after the impact; it is an inseparable component essential to the entirety of the swing. And applying the gestalt concept to the aspect of time, we can understand that the golf swing is really not made up of separate actions occurring in a linear sequence, but it is rather a "whole" event taking place as a *oneness*, not effectively being divided by separate aspects of time.

From *A Course in Miracles* perspective, this illusory world that we seem to be living in, as well as the individual bodies we appear to be inhabiting, all seem to be following a linear path through time, in a sequence of events that appears to have a past, a present, and a future we can't yet see. But the Course teaches that *there is no past,* and actually no "future," either. It is simply, *Eternity*, always.

This may be a hard concept to grasp, especially at first; but it becomes a little easier to digest when we think of the common understanding among most religions and spiritual paths that God knows the past, present and future. *It is all One to God!* And the Course tells us that we are One **with** God, and in our true state (our true reality), we share all that God is, and know all that God knows.

So this illusion that we currently seem to believe in tries to convince us (often *quite* convincingly) that we are indeed prisoners of, and limited by, the passage of time. But the truth is, we are not! In reality, we are still as God created us: perfect, changeless, and eternal. And as far as the concept of time goes, in Heaven (our real home, even at this very moment), it's *"Always now, all the time!"*

How does the concept of perfect follow-through enter into this?

Submitted for your approval: God's will for us is perfect happiness. God's will is that we share God's thoughts, constantly and completely. So any concept we have of totality, in *anything*, will naturally have to include the "whole" of that concept, and not leave any part of it excluded.

Sounds a lot like that "part" of the golf swing that comes after the striking of the ball, doesn't it? Even here in the illusory world, even as we seem to prepare to drive a golf ball down a fairway, we can still keep in mind the fact that in Truth (and at some level we are always aware of this), there is no *time* involved in our golf swing. It is all held within one single, complete, indivisible, eternal thought.

And God's will for us *is* perfect happiness. Therefore, God's will for us, which we always share, in truth – and which applies not only to our golf game, but also to our overall experience of life, and ultimately to our completely remembering the Oneness which is our true nature – God's will for us *is* perfect follow-through!

THE THIRD NINE

Hole 19

"I am determined to birdie."

(Inspired by A Course in Miracles: Workbook *Lesson 20)*

"I am determined to see."

The goal of the teachings of *A Course in Miracles* is to train ourselves to see the world through the vision of love rather than fear. To accomplish this, we must be determined to see things differently. To see things as they really are, we must be willing to release the past. Our ego mind has very limited vision and is always drawing from the past, and the past is a total illusion.

Think of a time when you accomplished something you were very proud of. *(Yes, I am asking you to go into the past!)* One of my favorite quotes from the Course is, *"All your past except its beauty is gone, and nothing is left but a blessing."* You can use your past to serve you, rather than keep you bound to the pain and limitations.

Let's say that you earned a college degree. To do this, you had a goal, chose a major, and followed the steps necessary to graduate, and were given that wonderful piece of paper handed to you as you walked across the stage! You were determined, and did whatever it took to accomplish your mission! Of course, there were challenges, and most certainly frustrations, but you had a goal, and you were determined to accomplish it!

The same holds true for vision. If you really want to see the world in its essence, its perfection, then set the intention, establish a goal, and do whatever it takes to accomplish it. The Course teaches us that if we really wanted the peace of God, we would have it. The truth is, we are so willing to throw it all away in exchange for meaningless musings. *In other words, we value the valueless!*

One of my favorite teachers of *A Course in Miracles* is Marianne Williamson. In her best-selling book *A Return to Love* (a must read for anyone who is new to ACIM), she has written a wonderful quote, which I along with millions of others find extremely empowering!

Our Deepest Fear

Our deepest fear is not that we are inadequate.
Our deepest fear
is that we are powerful beyond measure.
It is our light, not our darkness,
that most frightens us.
We ask ourselves,
Who am I to be brilliant, gorgeous, talented, fabulous?
Actually who are you not to be?
You are a child of God.
Your playing small doesn't serve the world.
There's nothing enlightened about shrinking
so that other people won't feel insecure around you.
We are all meant to shine, as children do.
We were born to make manifest

the glory of God that is within us.
It's not just in some of us; it's in everyone.
And as we let our own light shine,
we unconsciously give other people
permission to do the same.
As we're liberated from our own fear,
our presence automatically liberates others.

So many gems of truth are in this quote by Marianne. You were born to be great, you were born with a purpose! You were born to shine externally the light of God that is within you! Whether you are on the golf course, in the boardroom, or driving the carpool with the kids to school, God is with you. Sure, there will be moments where you are ready to explode, you feel as though nothing is going right, but in truth, all is perfect. Take a deep breath and ask for a miracle. Although the situation may not change, your perception will. You will experience a sense of peace that is not dependent on circumstances. This is what living *A Golf Course in Miracles* is all about!

We had an angel among us on this Earth for only a short time, but what a mark he left for us. *Mattie Stepanek.* Mattie was born with a rare disorder now known as Dysautonomic Mitochondrial Myopathy. His mother, Jeni, was able to see beyond his physical challenges, which allowed his spirit to soar. By nurturing his soul, Mattie wrote some of the most beautiful and inspiring poetry we have ever known.

Mattie became a bestselling author, publishing six collections of his *Heartsong Poetry*. One collection of Mattie's peace essays became a *New York Times* bestseller and eventually sold over two million copies. He gave inspirational talks to thousands and touched the lives of us all. His mother could have chosen to follow the doctors suggestions, and just let his illness take its course, but she did not, ***Thank God!***

How often do you sit back and let your life just "take its course?" How many times have you been paralyzed by fear? And why are you so fearful? Unfortunately, we are more programmed for failure than success, to be afraid rather than to love. It is time for us to step into our power! You have the power and potential to do great things! It's time to create a new paradigm. You can choose birdies over bogeys in every moment. It is time to demand birdies and eagles on the golf course and in your life! Only you can make the choices that will make this so. Are you determined to birdie? Yes? Then what are you waiting for???

In golf, *par* is good, a *birdie* is better, and an *eagle* is fantastic!

Actually, par is better than good. Par is not just "average" good; par is only average in terms of a **really** good outcome. If *everything* goes as it should, and each stroke is executed just the way it should be with no errors at all, then par will be the result.

So if a birdie is one under par, then that is an *exceptionally* good outcome…and an eagle, which is *two* under par? As they say on some golf courses in New Jersey: *"**Fuggedaboudit!**"* Remember; if you were playing a par-3 hole, and you ended up with an eagle on that hole, it would be because you had just gotten a *hole-in-one!*

So yes, an eagle in golf is something to crow about, indeed, and we'll spread our wings a little further regarding this high-flying idea in our next chapter, Hole 20. But here in Hole 19, we'll focus a bit more on why a birdie has anything to do with "seeing," and just what "determination" really means.

In golf, a birdie is *better than par,* and an outcome to be highly desired. In *A Course in Miracles*, we are taught about the differences between "seeing with the body's eyes," and **true** seeing, which

130

ultimately brings us to *vision*. True seeing, leading to vision, is *better* than seeing with the body's eyes, which can only show us images of an illusory world, and merely compound the illusion by making it look and seem believable to us.

When ACIM Lesson 20 tells us, *"I am determined to see,"* it is talking about this *better* form of seeing—the kind that shows us the truth, and the meaning behind symbols and illusions, rather than mere images of the illusions themselves. In Lesson 20 we are told, *"Your decision to see is all that vision requires... In your determination to see is vision given you."*

So it is *determination* itself that is what attainment of vision requires. This is reminiscent of a concept that we discussed back in our first "Hole" of *A Golf Course in Miracles: "I need par nothing,"* which was based on the *Course in Miracles* teaching, *"I need do nothing."* The basic principle being taught was that it is never the *doing* of any action (or the *parring* of any hole) that is the important factor in anything; it is always the *willingness* to be the observer, to allow things to be as they are rather than as we think we would like them to be that brings us the peaceful result we are seeking, whether on the golf course or anywhere else.

A Course in Miracles speaks about this concept of *willingness* quite often. It is not the "doing" of anything specific that is required in any given circumstance, but just the willingness itself, the willingness to turn things over, always, to the Holy Spirit, so that we can be guided to see things through *His* eyes, and not through the eyes of the ego. So the lesson *"I am determined to see"* is teaching us that it is not the "seeing" itself that is the critical requirement, but more importantly the *determination* to see.

And what does *determination* mean, precisely? The word itself contains within it the word, "termination," which refers to the end of something. In this case, it is intended to mean the end result of a decision process, a direction leading to a certain end, a definitive conclusion, a resoluteness, an ending of controversy. It goes beyond *tendency* and even *intention*; it indicates clearly a definitive decision to achieve a specified end result.

Therefore, the statement *"I am determined to see"* declares that it is my absolute decision to see in a better way than the body's eyes can ever show me, to see the reality that lies beyond all illusions, and to attain a state of vision that will show me the truth in all things and about myself as well.

And the *Golf Course in Miracles* lesson that *"I am determined to birdie"* is my declaration that I am determined to **exceed** par, and to always be willing and determined to achieve a *better outcome than average* in everything I encounter—on the golf course, in life, and even in my process of *spiritually awakening*…which is really just remembering the truth about who and what I really am!

Hole 20

"Above all else I want to eagle."

(Inspired by A Course in Miracles: Workbook *Lesson 27)*

"Above all else I want to see."

The more you allow yourself to practice these lessons and begin to experience the wonderful effects of your effort, life gets more fun! The stress and pain of day-to-day life challenges don't seem so big anymore. The really good news is that you have just begun, *and it only gets better!*

In the last chapter, "I am determined to birdie," we discussed that by making a decision and being vigilant and determined to birdie, your relationship to life and golf would radically change, *and it will,* with your commitment to making it so.

Now that you are experiencing the benefits from practicing these spiritual principles, you are thirsting for more. You realize that this stuff really does work! Your time on the golf course is much more enjoyable, you love your job, your kids are fabulous, and your spouse or partner doesn't upset you anymore! Keep it coming baby; this is just the beginning!

"Above all else, I want to eagle," is your new mantra! Par is a score that is determined by the yardage of each hole. Pars are wonderful, birdies (one under par) are great, and an eagle, (two under par) is out of this world! You were created for eagles! *A Course in Miracles* says that we feel like aliens in this world, because we are! This world we have made up is not our home! This world is limited on what it has to offer us. There is unlimited beauty and fulfillment waiting for you to accept it…but it is not where you think it is. Get off the wheel of suffering and surrender to the truth, which is pure potentiality. You are a child of God; it is time to act like it!

Once you make a decision to fly with the eagles, to transcend the limitation of this world, you have to be willing to let go. The weight of the burdens and worries you carry makes you too heavy to fly. Although you are living in this world, you do not have to live *"of"* this world.

There are literally no limits to what is possible, except in your mind. We are constantly inundated with the media and negative programming, which keeps us believing that we are limited. The same holds true with playing the game of golf. You have been programmed to believe that *if you are a certain age and physical condition,* then you can only go so far with your game. You may also think that eagles are not yours to have. As a teacher of golf, and metaphysics, **I know that is a lie!** There is no limit to your abilities on or off the golf course! *I am, however, also a realist.* By saying that, I realize that our programs and beliefs are very deeply rooted in our subconscious mind and that we have to identify and heal those beliefs before we can live to our highest capabilities.

How do you do this? Literally one thought at a time. You have thousands of thoughts in your mind in the course of a day. Most of them are from the past, and most are negative. Pay attention, be mindful, and choose love – love, not in the romantic sense, but rather in the sense of the unknown, the infinite – the eternal. Just as you train yourself to make a habit of good golf swing practices, you have the ability to train your mind to be much more than it has ever been.

Pars are good, birdies are better, and eagles...they are fantastic, but they are also just the beginning!

As Charlotte has stated, on the golf course, an eagle is *"out of this world!"* If a birdie is great, an eagle is that much greater still—a feeling of supreme accomplishment that almost can't be described. If it's true that, *"I am determined to birdie,"* with all that that implies, then when I state, *"**Above all else I want to eagle**,"* I am declaring my complete intention to soar to the very heights, beyond the normal expectations of the world, and to attain a state almost unimaginable from the perspective of my previous way of thinking!

An eagle is a pretty lofty goal, in the world of the golf course. And when *A Course in Miracles* tells us, in Workbook Lesson 27: *"Above all else I want to see,"* it is presenting us with a lofty goal as well. This is speaking of something beyond intention, beyond determination; we are stating that *"above all else,"* beyond **any** other concept, value, goal, or consideration, *"I want to see."*

To see must really be something! *"To see"*—to see truly and clearly, without distortion or illusion of any kind. To really *"get it,"* to no longer have the need to blindly subscribe to any belief system, or to have faith in things we can't really seem to understand...but simply, "to *know*," completely, accurately, and without doubt on any level. Yes, that is a lofty goal, indeed…and a goal that would surely be well worth attaining.

We are guided toward the pathway to this goal as the Course's lesson tells us, *"Today's idea expresses something stronger than mere determination. It gives vision priority among your desires."*

This idea "gives vision priority"…making the attainment of vision our *number one goal,* more important to us than *anything* else, beyond any other desires, other intentions, even beyond determination itself.

It is that commitment, that *willingness*, to have as our priority the attainment of something beyond the normal experience of the world that will allow this "change of thought," this *miracle*, to take place. Whether it is the attainment of true seeing, of total vision, or the achievement of playing an almost unimaginably successful hole on the golf course, it is our *willingness*, our determination, and *making it our number one priority* that will allow—will *compel*—that end result to occur.

It is reminiscent of Henry David Thoreau's oft-repeated quote: *"If one advances confidently in the direction of his dreams, and endeavors to live the life which he has imagined, he will meet with a success unexpected in common hours."* Thoreau is echoing the same message we are discussing here. *Advancing confidently,* and endeavoring to achieve that which we have envisioned – bringing into play both our intended desires, and our willingness to achieve them – will take us to heights unexpected in "common hours," i.e., in the commonly shared view of the world, and in our previous way of thinking.

But in our new way of thinking – thinking with the Holy Spirit's thought system, rather than that of the ego…and choosing to see not with the body's eyes, but with the true sight that actual vision will bring us – we can literally transcend the limitations of the world, its views, and its outcomes. And we will be able to actually see ourselves making that previously unimaginable *eagle*, as we make it our complete priority that, *"Above all else I want to see!"*

"I want to fly like an eagle, 'till I see,
Fly like an eagle, Holy Spirit carry me,
I want to fly like an eagle, to be free,
Oh, oh, here's a solution!"

(~with apologies to Steve Miller!)

Hole 21

"I can escape from the bunker I see by giving up hazard thoughts."

(Inspired by A Course in Miracles: Workbook *Lesson 23)*

"I can escape from the world I see by giving up attack thoughts."

The world we live in is not real. The world we live in is based on fear and limitation. There is nothing in this world that can come close to the experience of our true home, which is Heaven. In many of the world's religions, it is taught that Heaven is a destination where we can live for eternity if we are good little girls and boys while we are here. The streets are paved in gold, everyone is in their state of perfection, and we are with God! Sounds good to me, and certainly better than the alternative!

A Course in Miracles speaks of Heaven also, but from a little different perspective. The Course states that we are all going to awaken from the dream and remember our home in God, which is Heaven.

"Have faith in only this one thing, and it will be sufficient: God wills you be in Heaven, and nothing can keep you from it, or it from you."
ACIM: Text 249/268

Heaven and hell are states of mind, not a destination. Heaven is here now, just for the asking. In truth, we never have left the kingdom of God; we have just fallen asleep. In this dream, we believe that it is possible to be separate, but in reality, we cannot.

What keeps us here, is our attack thoughts, our judgments, our desire to be separate. To be fully at peace, we must be willing to include *everyone* in our circle in total love. Rather than seeing ourselves as separate from each other and blaming others and circumstances for our unhappiness, we must accept 100 percent responsibility for the world we see. The world you see is but a projection of yourself. If you see a world that is friendly and abundant, you are seeing a reflection of you. In other words, we see the world as we are! If you see a world that is fearful, and limited, you are also seeing a reflection of you. What does your world look like?

The Course states that all we must do is accept the atonement for ourselves, atonement being defined as the "undoing of fear." In truth, we are all one, so each time one of us chooses love over fear, *everyone* benefits by the gesture.

How does this relate to the sand trap, you may be asking? **A lot!** First, I am an excellent sand player. I love the sand, and I know that I am going to have a great shot to the pin from the sand, and guess what...*I do!* As an instructor of the game, I have noticed that the same does not hold true for most golfers. Sand is equated to fear! Once a player's shot has landed in the sand, any hope for a good score is gone in the golfers mind. The sand, also known as the "hazard," is a demon for many, and the outcome of the shot reflects the thoughts, beliefs, and feelings of the one hitting the shot!

Let's go back to the beginning of the hole. You are standing on the tee, evaluating the hole you are about to play. Where do your eyes go? What thoughts are you thinking? Very often, you are focused on where you do not want to go, and that for so many golfers includes the dreaded sand trap! The dominant thought you are holding before you take your shot is creating an energy and feeling in your body, which is sending a message to the bunker, *"Here I come!"* And you seem so surprised when your shot lands there. *Sound familiar?*

What the heck happened? You have yards and yards of fairway, and so little sand, but yet your ball seems to find it every time! The good news is that you can shift your thoughts, your feelings, and the "radar" to where your shot will land. Hazard thoughts will respond in kind; success thoughts will respond in kind as well.

The Law of Attraction is a law of the universe! Thoughts create your feelings and your feelings create a physical equivalent, just exactly as you have requested! Do you want to be in sand traps or the center of the fairway? Change your thoughts, change your world... *Literally!*

I was thinking just recently about what Charlotte has had to say regarding playing out of the sand, while I was watching a few minutes of professional golf's Match Play event on TV. It was near the end of the semifinal, and Bubba Watson was playing Martin Kaymer to determine who would advance in that competition. Watson needed to do well on this particular hole in order to remain competitive, and on one unusually challenging shot, he ended up in a fairway bunker. Still quite a long distance from the green, he also had to contend with the side edge of the bunker looming high above the level of the sand where his ball was lying.

I remembered Char's statement that, *"Sand is equated to fear!,"* and wondered how Bubba *(great name, isn't it?)* would respond to this situation. The ball was lying lightly atop the sand, which was the good news…but he had that bunker's high edge right in front of him that he needed to get over, and then still send the ball quite a distance down range to be anywhere near the green and the pin. The green itself was surrounded by bunkers of its own; so where Watson was located right at that moment would likely have seemed like a really scary situation for any player to be in!

And this is why the pros can do what they so often do. Bubba's shot scooped perfectly under the ball, lifting it out of the sand and carrying it just barely over the edge of the bunker, but still keeping the loft angle low enough that the ball got the distance it needed. It ended up right at the edge of the green in a narrow strip of grass separating the green from the greenside bunker next to it—just a short pitch away from the pin and the hole!

Unfortunately for Bubba, he didn't go on to win the overall match. But his masterful play on that hole, and not letting the fearful thoughts that might well have surfaced after landing in that sand trap get the better of him, allowed him to make a truly remarkable shot that fans will be talking about for a long time to come.

Bubba Watson didn't let any fear-based hazard thoughts prevent him from escaping from the bunker he seemed to see himself in. Let's take a look now at how our *A Golf Course in Miracles* lesson here in Hole 21 *("I can escape from the bunker I see by giving up hazard thoughts")* compares to the *Course in Miracles* lesson from which we take our inspiration *("I can escape from the world I see by giving up attack thoughts"),* and how we can apply these teachings not only to our golf game, but to our everyday lives.

First, let's compare *"the bunker I see"* to *"the world I see."* In golf, a bunker is a trap, often called a "sand trap." It's a place where you generally don't want to end up. Although, Charlotte tells us, *"I love the sand!,"* so it's really open to interpretation. If you don't see the sand as a problem, then a bunker doesn't feel so much like a trap to you! And to further the parallel, our teaching states "the *bunker* I see" where *A Course in Miracles* states, "the *world* I see." So there's a parallel here as well in the use of *bunker* as compared to *world*; and we might think of the world itself as a trap, if we were so inclined. The world can be a dangerous place, right? And short of interplanetary travel, there's no way to get off, other than death... isn't that true? So jeez Louise, if that doesn't sound like a trap, I don't know what does!

Unless...we decide to interpret it a different way, to choose again to see it all with a changed outlook. What some people see as a hazard, Charlotte and Bubba see as an opportunity for a great shot! Hazard thoughts or success thoughts – which ones do you want to experience the effects of?

And we can apply this also to the other parts of our lessons as well. Where we say, *"hazard thoughts,"* the Course says, *"attack thoughts."* It's a phrase often used in *A Course in Miracles.* The Course tells us that attack thoughts can refer to actually attacking someone or something, or to being attacked, or to even simply the concept of *being able to be attacked;* in other words, to be vulnerable to attack. This is not just a subtle difference that we are examining here; it is actually the key to understanding this concept.

"My attack thoughts are attacking my invulnerability," is the title of ACIM's Lesson 26, which then tells us, *"It is surely obvious that if you can be attacked you are not invulnerable."* Then later in that

143

lesson, it says, *"Because your attack thoughts will be projected, you will fear attack. And if you fear attack, you must believe that you are not invulnerable. Attack thoughts therefore make you vulnerable in your own mind, which is where the attack thoughts are. Attack thoughts and invulnerability cannot be accepted together. They contradict each other."*

So simply *thinking* thoughts of attack – and we could just as easily substitute for *attack* the words *hazard, suffering,* or *vulnerability* – just the *thinking* of those attack thoughts is the dynamic action that seems to make us vulnerable in our own mind, which is where our belief in our own state of being is determined. Once again, it is our thinking that determines our perception of our very reality.

The Course's Lesson 23 (upon which our chapter here is based) tells us: *"If the cause of the world you see is attack thoughts, you must learn that it is these thoughts which you do not want. There is no point in lamenting the world. There is no point in trying to change the world. It is incapable of change because it is merely an effect. But there is indeed a point in changing your thoughts about the world. Here you are changing the cause. The effect will change automatically."*

What then, actually, is the bunker I see? Is it a trap, a hazard, a place for me to experience vulnerability? If I can change the cause of what I see – which is to change my thoughts about that thing, that bunker, that obstacle to peace in whatever form it may ever take – then the effect will change automatically! When I choose to give up my "hazard thoughts," the things that used to seem like hazards will now appear as joyful opportunities.

The Course's Lesson 23 tells us, *"You are not trapped in the world you see, because its cause can be changed."* When we change our thoughts about bunkers or anything else, we realize we were never trapped in hazards of any kind, but always surrounded by endless possibilities for happiness!

<u>Hole 22</u>

"I do not perceive my own best handicap."

(Inspired by A Course in Miracles: Workbook *Lesson 24)*

"I do not perceive my own best interests."

Do you really think you know what is best for you? I am sure that you think you do, *but do you, really?* Probably not. You were born into this world, wide open, ready to experience all this planet has to offer. When you entered this *"classroom Earth,"* you were ambitious and ready to do it all! Depending on the family you chose to be born into *(yes, you chose that, too!)*, you were programmed by their beliefs, ideas, and ideals. Some of you, unfortunately, were not born into such a wonderful cocoon of love and nurturing. Either way, you were initiated into the beliefs of your surroundings.

Family, education, spiritual/religious, financial, geographical, political, and many other influences made you who you are today. Let's give everyone the benefit of the doubt and assume that they were giving to you what they thought was best for you. And let's assume, since this book is intended for golfers *(although it isn't, really)*, that you grew up in an upper middle class neighborhood, all of your comforts and needs were met, you had an opportunity for advanced education, and best of all, you were introduced to the game of golf! *Ahhh!* The American dream—golf at the local country club, a college education, luxury vacations, and the list goes on... You are one of the lucky ones! Just for fun, let's assume that was your experience and let's assume that all of these wonderful perks of life were given to you for your highest and best interest! Your parents, relatives, ministers, friends were all working on your behalf. Feels wonderful, does it not?

Let's put the shoe on the other foot. You were born into a family with little or no money, a college education was just a dream, your surroundings were less than happy, and you never traveled more than five miles from where you were born. *Golf?* Literally the last thought in your mind. Even more, a game thought to be for *elitist sissies!*

Either scenario, that of Cinderella, or that of her stepsisters, in truth, was all for your best interest. Regardless of what your situation was at birth and your developing years, *now* is all there is. The decisions you make each moment will move you in the direction of success or failure, war or peace, prosperity or poverty. Again, another example of how you must release the past, regardless of whether it seemed good or bad. Take from it what has served you to this moment, and let the rest go.

"Everything is for your best interests!" There are no exceptions to this law. Regardless of what lessons you have had, you have the choice to use them as opportunities to grow or to fail. It is your decision to make.

Of course, I would have to guess that we would all prefer to have the ideal childhood to look back on. Free of worries of money, knowing all of your needs are always met, and everyone around you was there to support you. Why would you choose anything else? Quite simply, to learn. Most likely, if you were to perceive your own best interests, you would choose those based on external means. We are taught and brainwashed to believe that *this* is good and *that* is bad. Even those who love us, *in all honesty*, believe that they are making decisions in our best interest. We do the same for ourselves, and carry it on to our friends, family, and children, all intended for love and well-being.

In the illusion, that is the way it is. However, we have no idea what our best interests are. We have ideas, we have beliefs—none of which are true. Our egos have no idea what our best interests are, *but Spirit does!* Which voice you follow is up to you.

Regardless of your past programs, you can change them, right now! None of them were good or bad, they just were. They were the lessons that were perfect for your highest and best good. *Now that you know better, you can do better!*

"I do not perceive my best handicap." As a young golfer, I could not wait to get a handicap in the single digits. And by the age of twelve, I did. I now realize, that every score I put into the computer, which gave back to me my current handicap, was all in my best interest. Of course, I always aspired to have a lower handicap, what golfer doesn't. But the real lesson was, and is, "What am I choosing to do with the handicap I have today?" Am I using it as an opportunity to assess and evaluate my game, my life, and do better? Or, am I using it to condemn myself and see myself as a victim?

The handicap system is a wonderful tool to see where your game matches up to the course rating, or par. It also is a tool to let you see where your game is compared to your playing partners. It is a leveler. When used properly, you can tee it up with anyone, and have a fair game. The same idea can be used in life. What is your handicap as a parent, employee, friend, or spouse? Are you a thirty-six or are you a scratch? Pay attention; be mindful, and ask your higher self for guidance. We are all meant to be scratch handicappers in life. Let Spirit show you how. Ask and it will be given, *but remember, your ego does not perceive your best interests!*

In *A Golf Course in Miracles*, we use golf situations and examples as metaphors for life. Our current chapter, "Hole 22," provides us with some great opportunities for exploration along these lines.

"I do not perceive my own best handicap." What is a handicap? The term is believed to have originated from the phrase, *"hand in cap,"* which had something to do with how wagering and the determining of odds took place back in the very old days—particularly where the wager or contest involved elements of unequal value or prowess. The term became widely applied to horse racing, both as far as determining the specific odds of winning for all the various horses involved in a race, as well as the possible applications of actual "handicaps" in the forms of additional weight added to the saddles of the faster horses, to even out their odds of winning with the rest of the field.

It is in this sense of the word that it is applied to golf. One player who is a *lot* better at the game than another is *always* going to beat the lesser player, so how can they ever compete together in a friendly game of golf? The answer lies in the handicap system. The lesser player carries a handicap number that has been assigned to him (based on the results of previous play), which gives him (or her) a certain point advantage before the game even begins. This is, in actuality, a handicap *against* the better player; the bottom line being that now the two of them should have an even chance of doing equally well in the results of any given game. As Charlotte described it, in the game of golf, the handicap is *"a leveler."*

What about life in general…and how does the concept of *"I do not perceive my own best handicap"* apply to this idea?

When we really think about it, no one "in life" is actually equal in his or her abilities and personal resources. People are taller, shorter, faster, slower, richer, poorer, smarter, not so smart… Everyone has their own challenges, which can sometimes be viewed as handicaps when compared to others. Then there are people with perceived physical or mental disabilities, who may be considered by some to be "handicapped." The point is, we all have various factors in our lives that either seem to lift us up or hold us down, and in some ways, the ones holding us down or holding us back can be seen, in a sense, as handicaps.

But what do we mean by saying, *"I do not perceive my own best handicap?"* What could possibly be meant by the phrase, *"best* handicap?"

If we are beginning to learn to see life from a higher perspective, where we come to realize that *everything* is for our own good, even the things that may seem to knock us down or hold us back at the moment – (remember that stuff about *"I am not the victim of the hole I bogey,"* and God being in my golf bag, and all that?) – then we have to recognize that even the things we may perceive as handicaps can actually be there for our benefit. The problem is, we usually don't recognize our best handicaps when they come along!

Back in my earlier days as a performing musician, I never really "made it to the big-time." Lack of finances, lack of serviceable equipment and transportation, lack of effective management…*some* cynics might say lack of superior singing and songwriting abilities, too—but that's better left for another discussion! Whatever the case,

149

it seemed like there were handicaps involved that kept me from achieving my early dreams of becoming a famous rock star.

But I see now that these were some of my *"best handicaps"*—I just didn't perceive them that way at the time! Had things actually *connected* in a big way for me way back then, and I became rich and famous… would I have found myself on the spiritual path that I eventually discovered? Would my life have become so focused on the money, the women, "living the rock star life," and all that generally goes with being famous at a young age, that I might never have found myself on the path that led me to *A Course in Miracles?* Would I have met my lovely wife, Helen, who is my soul mate and the love of my life? And would I have met all of the people in the spiritual community who are now my dear and beloved friends, including my wonderful co-author Charlotte…and, hence, *would this book that you are now reading even exist at all?*

This is starting to sound like an old *Twilight Zone* episode! Think about it: one smash hit single for old Gino back in the late sixties, and bye-bye, *A Golf Course in Miracles!*

But of course, even though I didn't perceive it as such at the time, *not* having that number one record (and all that would have followed along with it) was in actuality one of my **best handicaps**, and led me to all that has happily transpired since then.

(Here's a memorable point concerning how we relate to handicaps in life, and in golf, and how it is always just a matter of perception. I heard the beloved actor Michael J. Fox on a TV interview, where he made this terrific comment: *"I started playing golf in my forties, with Parkinson's disease… If that's not the definition of optimism, I don't know what is!"*)

The teaching from *A Course in Miracles* upon which our chapter here is based *(ACIM's Lesson 24: "I do not perceive my own best interests")*, begins by telling us this:

"In no situation that arises do you realize the outcome that would make you happy. Therefore, you have no guide to appropriate action, and no way of judging the result. What you do is determined by your perception of the situation, and that perception is wrong. It is inevitable, then, that you will not serve your own best interests. Yet they are your only goal in any situation which is correctly perceived."

In our current, apparent state – believing ourselves to be separated from God as well as from each other, and thinking that we are at the mercy of a frightening and uncaring world, filled with fear thoughts and apparent handicaps at every turn – our perception is not at all accurate. We see so little, and we can see from only such a tiny, isolated perspective, both physically as well as from the perspective of time! How could we possibly perceive our own best interests in any situation, when we can't possibly know all of the facts and variables involved? The *Course* tells us that when our perception is wrong, we will not know or serve our own best interests. And that perception will inevitably be wrong when we are seeing it from an illusory and limited state of being.

But in our *true state* – the one where we realize that we are always connected to our *True Source*, Who always perceives everything correctly and perfectly *(even from His perspective of being nestled comfortably in our golf bag as well as everywhere else)* – we can relax in the knowledge that whether we can perceive it accurately at the moment or not, we need not fear the outcome of any circumstance or situation, along with any apparent restrictions, disabilities, or disadvantages of any kind.

We can actually look forward to the surprising and joy-filled outcomes that will come our way, as long as we remind ourselves that, *"I do not perceive my own best handicap!"*

151

Hole 23

"I have invented the rough I see."

(Inspired by A Course in Miracles: Workbook *Lesson 32)*

"I have invented the world I see."

What a wonderful world we have created! Some of you may agree, and some of you may think quite the contrary. Whatever perception you may have of this world, one thing is certain; you invented it—not just some of it, but all of it! We are often happy to take credit for those things in our lives that we perceive as good, but when there is something we do not much care for, or dislike immensely, we want to assume no responsibility for it!

When I was playing competitive golf, I always loved being in the energy of the caddies. Caddies of forty years ago and the caddies of today are two different breeds of cat. If you are familiar with the character *"Bagger Vance,"* he was not so far off from some of the

153

caddies I grew up with. The caddies of my youth were wise, intuitive, and could read into a golfer, right to their soul. And, they were funny! Oh, the stories they could tell. The stories they shared about the 9-holers at the country club, to the tour player, could keep me entertained for hours.

The modern caddies have shifted with the game. They have become much more technological with their reading of the greens, yardages, and the course in general, but one element still holds true; to be good, they must be tuned into their player. It is like a marriage. The caddy and player are a team and the caddy sees the player's interests as important as his/her own. Not only because they will be handsomely rewarded for the player's success, but because they are truly connected.

I have recognized however, that often a caddy will be sharing the events of the day's round, and as they are giving their hole by hole, shot by shot blow of their round, it is not uncommon to say, "*We* had a great shot into the green on twelve," or "You should have seen that thirty footer with a double break *we* made on sixteen!" But, on the other hand, if the player had a terrible hole or shot, the caddies are always quick to note that, "You should have seen the awful shot that *John* hit on twelve today, *he* made a double bogey!" Or, "*Betty* could not read a single putt out there today!"

How quick and easy it is for us to want to take credit for all of the birdies and thirty footers in our lives, and take credit for others' successes as well, but how fast we want to separate ourselves from failure, both personally or collectively.

A Course in Miracles is a teaching that suggests we are responsible for the world we see—**ALL OF IT!** *(Just in case you missed that idea the other ninety-nine times I have mentioned it in the book!)*— not just the birdies and eagles, but the bogeys and beyond as well. We have invented it all! That also includes the rough!

154

The fairway, not the rough on the golf course, is our desired destination for our shots. We set up, take a swing, and where do we end up? In the rough. In life, we set up, give it our best swing, and where do we end up? In the rough! The fabulous news is, **"If you have invented the world you see, and you do not like it, you can change it!"**

We live in a world where there is duality. Black and white, good and bad, success or failure. In Heaven, there is only love; there is only God. Heaven is unconditional; it is neutral. There are no veils between us and love, between us and God. Here, in this world, we have a choice. We can choose which voice to follow: the ego, or the Holy Spirit. Just like putting your time in at the gym for a more fit body, or at the driving range to develop muscle memory for a better swing, the same holds true for your spiritual and mental musculature. The more you practice choosing love, the more you experience love. The more energy that you put into the fairway rather than the rough, that too will be your experience, because you now realize that you are creating it!

The world can be a rough place. So it's not just a coincidence that our Hole 23 from *A Golf Course in Miracles* is titled, *"I have invented the rough I see,"* and the lesson from *A Course in Miracles* (Lesson 32) from which our chapter here is inspired is titled, *"I have invented the world I see."* We offer the comparison between "world" and "rough" because in many ways the world is, in fact, much like the rough on a golf course.

In golf, the rough is not the *worst* place you could end up...but it's certainly not the best place, either. You'd much rather have your shot end up on the fairway, or better yet, on the green, rather than in the rough. But still, it's not the *worst* location; you might have ended up really off course, perhaps in the trees (or *behind* a tree), or in a bunker *(although, as we've already learned, for certain golfers like Charlotte McGinnis and Bubba Watson, apparently bunkers aren't always such a bad thing!)*, or you might have landed deep in a water hazard, which is a lousy result for *any* golfer.

So the rough is actually not the worst place to end up, but all in all, you'd really rather not be there. And this is very much like our status here on Earth. It's undoubtedly not the worst place in the universe; it's not as bad as that ice planet from the second **Star Wars** movie *(or that's the "fifth" movie, depending on how you choose to count them)*. Or, at the other end of the spectrum, it's not as bad as a world whose sun is gradually expanding and slowly incinerating all life on the planets that revolve in orbit around it. Surely, without question, there are far worse places to be than on Earth; but still, all in all, we'd really rather not be here.

That's because we'd rather be in *Heaven!* Now, I'm not talking about that place filled with clouds, where everybody has wings and wears togas, and plays harps all day…*although, that does sound like a good theme for a party!* But seriously, we're not talking about that traditional, "nice place but it might get a little boring after a while" view of heaven that most people generally think of.

We're talking here about **Heaven**, the *Real Deal*, the state of perfect, endless joy, of an existential peace that is beyond description, of the experience of an ever-expanding ecstasy of Light and Love…of a complete and eternal *Oneness* with God and all Creation.

Compared to that, Earth could seem like a pretty rough place!

The teaching from *A Course in Miracles* upon which our current hole/chapter is based is Lesson 32, *"I have invented the world I see."* The Lesson just prior to that one in the Course is Lesson 31,

"I am not the victim of the world I see," (which was the inspiration for our earlier chapter, *"I am not the victim of the hole I bogey."*)

These two Course lessons are indeed intended to be sequential, as Lesson 32 explains: *"You are not the victim of the world you see because you invented it. You can give it up as easily as you made it up. You will see it or not see it, as you wish. While you want it you will see it; when you no longer want it, it will not be there for you to see."*

The world we appear to see is "here in front of us" by our own choice. In actuality, it is here by our own invention!

In these Lessons, the Course tells us that we should apply this concept to both our *"inner and outer worlds, which are actually the same."* If everything we seem to see and experience is actually originating within our mind, then our inner experience quite literally *is* our outer experience, and we should, therefore, apply the same principle to both areas of thought. *Change your thinking; change your results!* The same principle that applies to your golf game applies to the whole world you think you see—the entire universe, in fact. Our "inner game" is always determining our outer game; what we are thinking will determine what we believe we perceive.

The rough may not be the worst place to be on the golf course, and planet Earth may not be the worst place to be in the universe. But neither of them are places where we would really choose to end up, if everything could be perfect. That's because what we are seeking *is* perfect – the condition which we already recognize, deep within each of us, as our true state, our actual reality – the state of Oneness and perfection in which we exist in our *True Home*.

And this is why, while we still seem to be spending time in this physical world, and perhaps occasionally playing a round of golf (or a game of any sort) while we appear to be here, we can learn a couple of related lessons from both the *Course* itself and *A Golf Course in Miracles*, too.

"I am not the victim of the hole I bogey," because, *"I am not the victim of the world I see."* And since, *"I have invented the world I see,"* I can also be assured that, *"I have invented the rough I see"*— and any other seeming obstacle I should ever come across, as well!

Hole 24

"There is no green my mashie niblick cannot reach."

(Inspired by A Course in Miracles: Workbook *Lesson 38)*

"There is nothing my holiness cannot do."

We live in a world of Big Berthas, hybrids and titanium. No, I am not speaking of large women, electric cars, or artificial knees, but rather golf clubs. *And*, the list goes on and on. Just like so many things in our world, technological advancements continue to make the game of golf and the game of life easier! Golf balls are entities unto themselves! They are made up of so many composites and dimple designs, you need a degree to understand what is going on.

In my early days of playing the game, *(and I do not consider myself old by the way),* I had eighty, ninety, one hundred compression balls to choose from—Surlyn (hard cover) and balata (soft cover), and only a few brands available. Of course, I always desired and coveted the "Cadillac" of golf balls, *Titleist!* Today, there are literally hundreds, if not thousands of options to choose from. For clubs, the same is true. My clubs from forty years ago, compared to the clubs of today, look like "tinker toys!"

In ancient golf, BC, *(before Charlotte),* shafts of golf clubs were made of wood. Often, they were crafted by hand, many times by the actual players themselves, and really exhibited no standardized forms or shapes. As the game of golf developed into a bona fide sport, a "regular set" of clubs started to become the norm, with individual clubs being designed to accomplish specific tasks and hit a variety of different shots. As time went on, more workable iron came into general usage for shorter-range clubs, leading to an ever-widening variety of clubs becoming available.

I love the names that were given to clubs of the past. *The woods were named brassie, spoon, and baffling spoon.* Today we identify our woods not by naming them, but rather by numbers. Although identified today by numbers, the irons of old were named as well—*cleek, mid mashie, mashie, mashie niblick, pitching niblick, and so on!*

The *"mashie niblick"* was the historical golf club, wooden-shafted and used primarily before the twentieth century, that would be most closely associated with today's 7-irons. I used to "love" my 7-iron, a.k.a. my *"mashie niblick."* It was my *secret weapon,* and when I had it in my hands, I knew I could do anything! I still remember a shot I hit while playing with my father and a friend of his. I was on the fourth hole at the club in West Virginia I grew up on. I was about 160 yards from the green, and had a blind shot over some very large trees to the pin. I pulled out my 7-iron *(mashie niblick),* took my best swing, and like magic, I landed two feet from the hole! I was delighted, and my father and his friend were amazed. I was about eleven years old at the time and I was not supposed to be able to do that!

I share this story because besides the fact that it was a great shot, there were many more elements at play here. I was eleven, my clubs were technologically inferior to what is available today, and most likely, my ball that I was using was something from K-Mart that my dad had given me. And yet, today, with the best technology, I do not think I could repeat the shot. Not because I am close to fifty years old, but rather I have gathered so much useless information that has created a distraction from me and my best golf.

So often, we can think ourselves into becoming paralyzed. To play our best golf, or live our best life, we must be free of mind chatter. When we are free of the "monkey mind," then we are making space for the inner game to come forth! There is a "fine line" between the inner game and taking advantage of all of the wonderful resources of information and technology available to us. Remember, the world you see is totally a projection of your own inner game.

My 160 yard shot with my little *"mashie niblick"* over the trees, was one free of fear. Live free of fear and live well!

* Historical Note: Way back when, in the land of golf's birth, the Church of Scotland frowned upon its members playing golf on Sundays. So enterprising golfers came up with the idea of what came to be known as "Sabbath Sticks!" These were golf clubs made to look like common walking sticks. They were held upside down, with the club head fitting into the golfer's palm while walking. Then, when reasonably certain of being unseen by any disapproving church authorities, the club would be reversed, and a few clandestine strokes of golf could be played!

OK, we admit it; this chapter is really just a *gift* for those old-school traditionalists who remember a time when golf clubs were identified by names instead of numbers!

For those who may not be up on their ancient Scottish golf terminology, a mashie niblick is, as Charlotte described, approximately the equivalent of a modern-day 7-iron *(or perhaps, according to various other sources, somewhere between a 7-iron and a 9-iron).* The specifics aren't all that important, especially considering that way back then, there were really no specific standard requirements for clubs at all! It is important to remember that back in the *good olde days* there was no actual golf club manufacturing industry; clubs were generally made, one at a time, by blacksmiths, furniture makers, and other independent craftsmen (and probably a few enterprising crafts*women,* as well!)—or, as Char said, many times clubs were simply fashioned by the players themselves. So it is undoubtedly safe to say that any one mashie niblick of the time was very likely *not* exactly the same as any other mashie niblick. *(And so much for even the notion of standardized loft angles!)*

The idea here in *A Golf Course in Miracles* is that a mashie niblick is a wonderful *symbol* for something old and traditional, something that has stood the test of time, and proven itself worthy and useful.

In a way, that's very much like, "our holiness."

Our *AGCIM* hole/lesson here, *"There is no green my mashie niblick cannot reach,"* is inspired by *ACIM* Lesson 38, *"There is nothing my holiness cannot do." Nothing!* Our holiness is all-powerful and, hence, is both worthy and useful...and being truly *eternal,* it is superior to and completely *beyond* any test of time.

The concept of our inherent holiness is discussed in several earlier lessons from *A Course in Miracles.* We are told that the idea of our being holy *"does not describe the way you see yourself now."* (And it's *this* way of thinking we are now learning to change!) It is further

162

explained that, *"You are holy because your mind is part of God's."* We have already described here in this book that God is "in our golf bag," meaning that God is within us, in our mind; our inseparable connection to God being right there in our arsenal of tools to be used for any circumstance—on the golf course or anywhere else. If God is holy *(and we can certainly assume this to be the case!)*, and if God is "with us" *(in our minds, our golf bags, and everywhere)*, then God's holiness must be one with us as well.

The mashie niblick is our symbol for a proven, useful, trustworthy, ages-old device for taking us from where we appear to be currently located along the path, to where we want to be, to the area that is our true goal.

In golf, the green is our goal from the fairway, just as Heaven is our real goal from the perspective of where we seem to be in the world. The mashie niblick is the tool we use, proven to be useful, to reach the green…just as our holiness is the "tool" that guarantees our ability to reach our Heavenly goal. In fact, we've never actually left our perfect condition of Oneness with our Creator and with all that has been created; but our **holiness**, the **mashie niblick** of our spiritual arsenal, will absolutely enable us to re-awaken to our True State.

*There is no goal it cannot reach, and **nothing** it cannot do!*

163

Hole 25

"Let me not forget my divot."

(Inspired by A Course in Miracles: Workbook *Lesson 64)*

"Let me not forget my function."

This is the chapter where we get to explore the etiquette of the game of golf. Golf has always been described as being a *"gentlemen's game,"* a game of honor and respect. From the first time I stepped foot on the golf course, the rules and etiquette of the game were instilled in me. I was taught to replace my divots, fix ball marks on the greens, and rake the sand traps after I was finished. It was also brought to my attention to be courteous to my playing partners, never talk while they are hitting their shots and to acknowledge any well-executed shots with a kind remark.

Twenty-first century golf is a game I do not recognize in many ways. Back-to-back tee times where carts are lined up with golfers anxiously awaiting to tee off, divots and ball marks not being repaired, and sand traps left unattended with giant footprints waiting for the next golfer to land in, do not reflect the game of my youth! Manners, courtesy, and honor for your playing partners are not as obvious as they were in the past. I see players cursing the group in front of them to pick up their pace, and no regard for the rules and discipline of the game.

I love to walk and carry my bag when I play. As a child, it was a treat when we got to ride in a cart, but now, it is not my preference. I appreciate so much the purity and history of the game, and so much of it has been lost.

A few years back, while vacationing in California, I thought I would take a shot at getting a tee time at Pebble Beach. It had always been a dream of mine to play there, so I made the call. To my surprise, and delight, there was a tee time available for a single to play. I immediately jumped into the car with a friend who I was traveling with and made the beautiful drive to Pebble Beach.

I had no clubs with me, so I rented them. I bought balls, a glove, and in my tennis shoes, I was ready to go. Pressed for time, I ran to the first tee without hitting a single ball to warm up (which is not my usual practice). By the time I got there, my group of three men was already on the green. The starter set me off to catch up with them, and I literally hacked my way down the first fairway. As I was catching my breath, I finally reached the green. I introduced myself, put out my hand, and barely got a response. This is going to be interesting, I thought to myself. Thank God I had my friend with me to talk to, otherwise, I would have been talking to the birds and the sea otters!

On the next tee, I joined them on the men's tees and they told me the *"ladies' tees"* were up ahead. I responded kindly by saying; *"I was in a hurry trying to catch up with you guys on the last hole, so my best shots were not reflected, but I really do know how to play this game, thank you!"* I never did share with them I was a pro.

As the round progressed, I got better, and they got worse. I was beating them by a large margin and their moods were becoming grumpier. Every time the beverage cart would come, they would indulge in more cocktails, making their chance of playing well less than good. I had the pleasure of watching them "pee" from the side of their carts and beat their clubs into the ground in frustration. Needless to say, their approach to the game and mine were miles apart.

When I stepped onto the 18th tee, I had goose bumps! I had seen my golfing idols on television many times play this hole in major championships. The Pacific Ocean in the background was breathtaking, and I realized that *I was now on hallowed ground!* The 18th at Pebble Beach is a par 5. I hit a great drive; my second shot was in position for me to approach the green in three. I pulled out my 7-wood and hit a shot only three feet from the hole! ***I made a birdie!*** I was a happy girl, and grateful for the day's experience.

The fellows I was playing with stormed off the green, jumped into their cart without ever saying a word, never to be seen again.

Their caddy, who had been kind all day, said nice words about my game, and congratulated me on my birdie on 18. When we got back to the clubhouse, the caddy shared with the pro highlights from my round, and was very complimentary of my game. The next question from the pro to me was, *"Did you beat them?"* When I said yes, he could not have been happier. He then proceeded to tell me that when my group found out they were playing with a woman, they had a fit and demanded a meeting with the professional staff and management of Pebble Beach. They made it known that they did not spend several hundred dollars each to play Pebble Beach with a woman! They were told that Pebble Beach was a public golf course and that they had no choice in the matter. They then took off down the first fairway without me. Good thing I did not know this till after the round! The pro then said, we all prayed that you would beat them, and you did! *I have to say, my ego was feeling pretty good at the time!*

If by chance if any of you boys are reading this, and I hope you are, I want to let you know that I forgot to tell you that I was a pro! (OOPS, Sorry!) OK, I will admit it, I still have a little bit of *p___ and vinegar* in me! But as the lesson says, "Let me not forget my function," and what is my function? To forgive. Not in the sense of making them wrong and taking a spiritually superior role and saying "I forgive you," but rather taking full responsibility for my vision and decision to see them as anything less than perfect. So, the appropriate response to these wonderful children of God with whom I had the honor of playing golf is, **"Thank You!"**

When you are tempted to attack or defend, justify your anger or exempt anyone from your foursome, say quietly to yourself, *"Let me not forget my function (or my divot)!"*

Charlotte's tale about playing golf at legendary *Pebble Beach* is absolutely terrific (as well as hilarious!), and illustrates a perfect example of the message of *A Course in Miracles:* that it is indeed possible, and in truth it is our function, to always remember that we are "in the world but not of it." We can, in fact, still rather wholeheartedly enjoy the comeuppance bestowed upon a group of rude and self-centered golfers (or, for that matter, a group of *any* people doing *whatever* it is that offends us), while at the same time still seeing them as the perfect creation of God, just as we are...and as deserving as we are of forgiveness, too.

In fact, one of the secrets of the forgiveness process is that it's really *easier* for us to forgive others; we are generally too hard on ourselves, and too unwilling to let ourselves off the hook for what we think we have done wrong. It is when we begin to see that *as we see others, so do we see ourselves,* that we begin to realize that since we all come from the same source, we are all part of the Oneness of perfect creation...and, therefore, we are all equally worthy of forgiveness.

A Course in Miracles teaches us in its Workbook Lesson 64 (from which our current *AGCIM Hole* is inspired), *"**Let me not forget my function.**"* It says, *"The purpose of the world you see is to obscure your function of forgiveness, and provide you with a justification for forgetting it."* The world we seem to see around us was designed by the ego for the precise purpose of making us think we are actually a part of it! The *truth* about us is so very far beyond the petty concerns and limitations of this illusory world...yet the ego has set everything up so that we will think we see exactly the opposite of that Truth.

"It is only the arrogance of the ego that leads you to question this," the Course tells us of that truth. And this is where the process of **forgiveness** comes into play; forgiveness is the means by which we can actually shift our thinking from that of the ego (and all that it would have us believe) to the thinking of the Holy Spirit—which is actually our real thought system, anyway. Our inseverable connection to the Holy Spirit provides us with the means to *choose again*, this time to see the world for what it really is—the illusion of the ego—and in doing so, to now use that illusion to actually free ourselves from it!

"To the Holy Spirit, the world is a place where you learn to forgive yourself what you think of as your sins," the Lesson tells us. What was designed to enslave us – the apparent reality of the world, of our existence as individual, separated beings, and of the grievances we believe we have perpetrated upon ourselves and each other – all of this can be used under Spirit's direction to dissolve those illusory beliefs that have kept us bound by the ego's game plan up until now. And we can begin to play a bigger game—a *better* game, and one in which we *All* come out as winners.

*"**Let me not forget my divot**,"* is the title of our Hole 25 here in *A Golf Course in Miracles*. Are we drawing a parallel between our

169

"function" and "divots"? Well, in a way, yes. We have been taught that our function is forgiveness; and we forgive grievances, errors... the perceived "trespasses" of others (as well as our own.) So what's the deal with the divots?

Divots are, of course, those chunks of grass and sod that get scraped up and sent flying when striking a golf ball, usually occurring on the fairway. A divot is not really unexpected; they happen all the time, and they are actually just an anticipated side effect of many well-hit fairway shots. Divots are not considered transgressions, flaws, or even errors, and should not result in any grievances to be forgiven. They are not actually any form of "trespassing." *(This is assuming that you actually have permission to be playing on the golf course where this occurs!)*

Still...a divot *does* tear a chunk of turf out of the golf course (which the grass itself may not be too pleased about), and in a way, it leaves a disturbance—a scar—as a result of its passage. So while a divot is not anything *wrong*, it's still kind of...not *right*, in a sense, either! So what does the responsible golfer do about it?

We remember the words, *"Let me not forget my divot!"* We take that scooped-out piece of turf and carefully place it back where it had been, looking all nice and pretty, and hopefully ready to reattach its own root system and resume its grassy function on the fairway.

(Many courses in the South use bermudagrass, and in those cases divots are repaired by filling them in with a green sand/fertilizer mixture instead of using the original piece of turf. But either way, the purpose is the same—to restore the fairway grass back to its original condition.)

The grass has its own function in the illusion of the golf course and in the world, and we have our function, too: *to forgive!* To forgive everything we seem to see within the illusion of the world—the grass, the divots, the other golfers (rude or well-mannered), as well as ourselves and every other brother and sister we seem to see walking this world with us. Yes...none of this is real, and so in truth, there's really nothing to forgive. But we still seem to think we see these things; therefore, forgiveness, as our function, provides the principle and the means by which we will see the truth beyond them all.

And just as our divots are not really transgressions or trespasses, but just the anticipated side effects of playing the game of golf, so are all of the grievances we appear to encounter just the expected side effects of seeming to be living in this illusory world. And yet our lesson teaches us to handle them both in the same way: by *never forgetting* our function—or our divots!

Hole 26

"God is the caddie with which I play."

(Inspired by A Course in Miracles: Workbook *Lesson 45)*

"God is the Mind with which I think."

As I mentioned earlier, the value of a good caddie cannot be over-stated. The player/caddie relationship is a partnership. The player depends upon his or her caddy for yardages, reading of greens, replacing divots and ball marks, raking the traps, but most impor-tant, caddies help their player to maintain emotional control on the course. Once any golfer allows their anger or negative emotions to take over, they have thrown their game to the wind. A good caddy is willing to take the blame where there is none, just to support their player. Tour caddies who are on the bag of a top player are well paid for what they do. *Many of them can make upwards of six figures in a year. (In a **perceived** bad economy, might not be a bad job to consider!)*

Needless to say, a great caddy is invaluable, and many tour players will have the same caddy with them for the better part of their career.

Obviously, I have established the value of a good caddy. But what about allowing yourself to have the top caddy, the caddy of all caddies? *"Who is that? Sign him or her up!"* The good news is, you already have the caddy to which I am referring with you always. That is because *"God is with you wherever you go!"* In truth, you are never separate from God; you just think that you are.

"God is the mind with which I think," refers to your true mind, your infinite mind! When you choose to plug into the mind of God, you will be at peace; you will see the possibilities rather than the obstacles. It is your decision, which mind you choose. Why would you choose to play small when all of the universe is yours to tap into? Most likely, it is fear of loss. You may think that if your ego gives up control, then you will not get what you want. *Do you really know what you want?* Sure, you think you do, but it is doubtful that you do. All of the meaningless attempts to find value in this world will always fail. *A Course in Miracles* states that it is a very strange belief that we have made, to believe that our will and God's will for us can be separate.

Sure, a fabulous caddy is invaluable. But make sure you allow the **presence of possibility** to be included in the game. The results will astound you! Peace, joy, and hope will be with you for every shot, every round, and every moment. Who's *your* caddy?

That God…He's one busy Creator, isn't He? I mean, think about it; there He *(or She)* is (at least according to our book *A Golf Course in Miracles*), in every green we see, in our golf bags, and even caddying for us! A regular "Jehovah of all trades", by whatever name you choose to refer to Him. And I'm sure (at least hypothetically speaking) that in His role as our caddie, if we were to hit a really lousy golf shot and angrily responded with a certain all-too-common phrase about it, He might admonish us by saying, *"No, I will not actually damn that golf ball as you have requested!"*

Yeah, that's God—always taking a *Superior* attitude!

But all kidding aside, God really can be thought of as our ultimate caddie. Why? Because God is in every green we see, in our golf bags, in everything we see and think of. God is in everything because God is in us, and we are in God. We share the Oneness of God; we share it with God, and with each other. This Oneness has nothing to do with our physical bodies, which are part of the illusory universe, and are, therefore, the result of the ego's thinking. Our Oneness with God results from our being the extension of God, and is why we all share, and indeed are part of, the Mind of God.

A Course in Miracles Lesson 45 (from which our Hole 26 here in this book is inspired) is titled, ***"God is the Mind with which I think."*** This is referring once again to the *real thoughts* that we think with God, as opposed to the illusory thoughts of the ego (which the Course tells us we only "think we think".)

In the practice of the Course's Lesson, we are instructed to *"try to go past all the unreal thoughts that cover the truth in your mind, and reach to the eternal."* Again, we are presented with the concept that time itself is part of the illusion of the ego; in the Oneness of our perfect creation we are in eternity, always. In truth, it is always "now," as we have discussed previously here in this book.

That *Course in Miracles* lesson goes on to tell us, *"Under all the senseless thoughts and mad ideas with which you have cluttered up your mind are the thoughts that you thought with God in the beginning. They are there in your mind now, completely unchanged. They will always be in your mind, exactly as they always were. Everything you have thought since then will change, but the Foundation on which it rests is wholly changeless."*

The Course's deep metaphysics are reminding us that, ultimately, only that which is entirely changeless—entirely *eternal*—is of God, and is therefore real. Anything that can change, shift, be altered or damaged, suffer or die, must by definition be a result of the thinking of the ego...not of God. And we are "of God," and God's is the Mind with which we think—for real.

Here in *A Golf Course in Miracles*, our goal is always to apply these deeper concepts in ways that can benefit us while we still seem to be here on planet Earth—practical solutions whereby these principles can be applied to our golf game, as well as to any and all aspects of our human lives. So how does the idea of *"God as caddie"* fit into this arrangement?

A golfer's caddie has some physical responsibilities, such as carrying the golf bag, replacing divots, raking sand traps...but the true value of a good caddie is, as Charlotte explained, the judgment, experience, and intelligence that the caddie can bring to the game for the benefit of the player. Helping the golfer make critical decisions, and also maintain emotional control during the game (as Char emphasized) is really what makes a superior caddie truly worthy of high praise!

So, Who better to do all of that (and receive all of that praise) than the *ultimate caddie:* God! (All right, God really doesn't care at all about that praise business, quite honestly. He obviously already knows how cool and powerful He is without having to hear us sing loudly about it. Still, after the thoughtfulness of putting on His caddie outfit and playing the round with us, maybe we should cut Him some slack and sing Him a little praise anyway...*you know, for the effort!)*

But seriously, think about it; we are connected to God, always. The Holy Spirit (God's eternal communication channel to us) is always there, always ready to help us *choose again* to think with our "real mind," and not with the ego. All of the corrected judgment, infinite intelligence, emotional guidance and support – and the constantly renewable resource which is the insurmountable *power of forgiveness* that enables us to change our thinking about *anything* we appear to encounter – all of this is ours, to bring along with us on every golf course and with every step we ever take upon this or any other world…as long as we never fail to remember that, *"God is the caddie with which I play!"*

Hole 27
"I am entitled to mulligans."

(Inspired by A Course in Miracles: Workbook *Lesson 77)*

"I am entitled to miracles."

Wouldn't it be wonderful if every time you hit a poor shot on the golf course you could take it over without a penalty? It always tickles me to see a golfer when they miss a shot and before the ball even lands, they are reloading to hit another one! *Not that there is anything wrong with wanting to take a mulligan...* I have noticed however, that mulligans are usually the better shot. *Why is that?* You throw down your ball, swing without a thought or plan in mind, and all of a sudden, you hit a fabulous shot! When you approach a shot with an empty mind, and release stress in your body, you are making a space for the perfect shot to come forth. *(Just in case you were not sure of the rules, in an actual game of golf where you are keeping score, mulligans are not allowed!)*

In 1981, I played a golf marathon on the Champion Course at PGA National Golf Club in Palm Beach Gardens, Florida. It was a benefit for programs for junior golfers. The more holes I played, the more money I raised. I managed to play 216 holes in one day, averaging fifty minutes a round. I had a support team with me and they kept score. My average score was 74 for the twelve rounds of golf, and that was on a very challenging course, *and* without any mulligans!

Needless to say that when you are averaging fifty-minute rounds, (less than three minutes a hole), you do not have much time to think. I literally was looking at the shot and creating it in my mind as I was approaching it, got a picture of my desired outcome, set up, and took a swing. I was playing from my *inner game.* I had no thoughts, but rather a clear picture of where I was going. I am not suggesting that this would have been possible without the prior years of training and practice, but on that day, I literally did not have a thought in my mind—I was free!

Think about when you play, do you have too many thoughts going on in your mind? You may want to pay closer attention to professional athletes, dancers, or musicians. When you are observing anyone who is a master of their field, they are performing from their "Zen" mind, a.k.a. the "zone."

"I am entitled to miracles." Yes, you are, and so is everyone else! A miracle, or shift in perception is yours for the asking. In life, I am sure we all would like to take a mulligan or two. You absolutely can, *because your past is gone.* Why are you creating the same patterns over and over again? **Because you didn't get it right the first time.** When your *"mulligan,"* or *"do over"* shows up in your life, make a decision to respond differently—choose the miracle. I am a believer that there are no limits to anyone's potential. The only limits we have are those that are in our minds and in our beliefs. By choosing a different guide, meaning your higher self over the ego, you are choosing the miracle, and it is much more fun to live in *miracle land* than in the pain of the ego!

You are entitled to miracles and mulligans. Choose wisely!

The term "mulligan" means a do-over, a chance to try something once again, and hopefully get it right this time. The word itself sounds rather Irish, of course *(Faith and Begorrah!)*, and there are several theories as to where it originated; most sources admit that the theories and stories about this are very likely not true. But who cares? It's commonly understood, especially in the world of golf, that a mulligan is a do-over.

And, as Charlotte said, mulligans are not technically allowed in golf... when one is actually playing by the official rules, at least. Still, in many "friendly" games, allowing mulligans has been agreed on by the players involved, so it's OK with them; and there are even some charity events where mulligans are "sold" by the organizers to raise funds for the charitable cause. So while mulligans are not technically allowed as part of the game of golf, they certainly pop up "unofficially" on golf courses all the time.

In fact, if your fellow players in a friendly round of golf allow you to take a mulligan when you've really shanked a bad drive, you might consider that to be somewhat of a minor miracle! But what do *real miracles* and mulligans have in common? Our Hole 27 here in *A Golf Course in Miracles* is titled, *"I am entitled to mulligans,"* and is inspired by ACIM Lesson 77, *"I am entitled to miracles."* So what is the connection?

As we've said, a mulligan is a do-over – the opportunity to correct a mistake, to do something once again, and to get it right this time. The miracle, as the Course defines it, is a *change of mind*, a correction of our thinking, a changing over from the thought system of the ego to that of the Holy Spirit. Until now, we have been following the ego's thinking, perceiving ourselves to be isolated, endangered, and separated from our Creator. The miracle – which can really be thought of as a "metaphysical mulligan" – allows us a do-over, the opportunity to choose our preferred thought system once again… and yes, to get it *right* this time!

In Chapter 31 from the Text of *A Course in Miracles*, we are taught that in every difficult and stressful situation, whenever we question the perplexity of what we appear to be up against, our inspired guidance will always tell us that the answer is, *"My brother, choose again."* (That applies to *sisters*, too!) Through thinking with the ego, we have created an image of ourselves as what we are **not**, and have essentially rejected the reality of what we really are. The Course tells us, *"The images you make cannot prevail against what God Himself would have you be. Be never fearful of temptation, then, but see it as it is; another chance to choose again…"*

"Choose again" – that's the miracle, the *mulligan of the mind* that lets us see ourselves as One with our Creator and with each other – perfect, whole, and incapable of being threatened, harmed, or damaged in any way. Another excerpt from the Course's Text also tells us, *"You are as God created you, and so is every living thing you look upon, regardless of the images you see. What you behold as sickness and as pain, as weakness and as suffering and loss, is but temptation to perceive yourself defenseless and in hell. Yield not to this, and you will see all pain, in every form, wherever it occurs, but disappear as mists before the sun. A miracle has come…"*

Our current hole/chapter in *AGCIM* is inspired by *ACIM* Lesson 77, *"I am entitled to miracles."* The word "entitled" is a key concept; we do not just receive or have access to miracles…we are **entitled** to them! *"You are entitled to miracles because of what you are,"* that lesson teaches us. *"Your claim to miracles does not lie in your illusions about yourself. It does not depend on any magical powers* *you have ascribed to yourself, nor on any of the rituals you have devised. It is inherent in the truth of what you are."*

"Today we will claim the miracles which are your right, since they belong to you," Lesson 77 continues. *"You have been promised full release from the world you made. You have been assured that the Kingdom of God is within you, and can never be lost. We ask no more than what belongs to us in truth."*

"Ask no more than what belongs to us in truth." That line has always reminded me of something another wise philosopher once said. It was Sally, from the comic strip "Peanuts," who declared in the classic *A Charlie Brown Christmas*, "All I want is what I have coming to me! All I want is my fair share!"

And you know, Sally had it right. The miracle *is* what we have coming to us; the miracle is our fair share. The miracle is the change of thinking that we always have open to us, always available to allow us to shift from the limited, defeated, painful and fear-based thinking of the ego, to the limitless joy and endless possibilities that the thought system of the Holy Spirit provides us.

We are entitled to miracles, and we are entitled to mulligans! The miracle is the definitive do-over, the *ultimate mulligan;* it is our endless right to change our thinking at any and every moment, and to *choose again*—this time, knowing beyond doubt that we will absolutely get it right!

THE REAL 19TH HOLE

The Real 19^(TH) Hole
(A.K.A. THE FINAL SCORE)
28: "I could see the clubhouse instead of this."

(Inspired by A Course in Miracles: Workbook *Lesson 34)*

"I could see peace instead of this."

Give yourself a pat on the back! You have just completed twenty-seven holes/chapters in *A Golf Course in Miracles!* Let's head up to the clubhouse and have a bite to eat and a drink, and share a few of the "gems" of your round.

The purpose of this book is twofold: to offer suggestions and ideas to help you enjoy the game of golf *and* life more. If you will apply the lessons in your life, I promise you that you will experience more peace and joy both on and off of the golf course.

I encourage you to take these lessons with you on the golf course.

When you hit a poor shot and are tempted to be angry, say to yourself, "I can choose peace instead of this."

If you are paired with a group that you do not particularly care for, instead of complaining or not showing up, make a commitment to see past your perceived judgments and ask your higher self to be your eyes.

Practice being in the present moment; release the past. Put your attention on your desired outcome rather than on your past experience. Remember, what you focus your thought on becomes your reality.

You are 100 percent responsible for the world you see. The good news is that if your life is not what you desire, you have the power within you to change it!

A Golf Course in Miracles is a course in mind training. This is just the beginning of your journey, not the end. You are the one swinging the club, and you are the only one who can call the shots!

My prayer for you is that your life is filled with birdies, eagles, and miracles in every moment.

Choose Well!

There it is: the beautiful, inviting room...perhaps paneled in dark, rich wood, elegantly carpeted, replete with an inviting bar, and comfy cushioned seats. Cooling breezes from the overhead ceiling fans...or maybe the warmth of a crackling fire (depending on the weather conditions outside.) Most likely some refreshing beverages and perhaps a selection of tasty, festive snacks as well.

The perfect place to relax, unwind, and discuss the events of the day and of the now-completed game with a group of close friends and acquaintances. This is *the Clubhouse*...

Peace! Or in other words: *'Heaven'*.

It can certainly feel like Heaven to shed the cares of the world and of competition, and to truly relax. No stress, no worries, no demands or requirements...everything just as it's supposed to be.

We're 'home'...we're at peace...we're in Heaven.

This is the *Clubhouse* we envision in *A Golf Course in Miracles*. It is a state of mind...and it is one we can have at any moment, in any circumstances. The title of this, our final hole in AGCIM, *"I could see the clubhouse instead of this,"* is inspired by *A Course in Miracles* Lesson 34, *"I could see peace instead of this."*

The relaxing mindset of the clubhouse is an example of the peace that we can choose at any time, under any conditions. The Course's lesson tells us, *"It is from your peace of mind that a peaceful perception of the world arises."* We are also given a phrase to practice as an exercise, whenever anything should arise that threatens to disturb our peace of mind: *"I could see peace in this situation instead of what I now see in it."*

These teachings really sum up what we have been presenting here in *A Golf Course in Miracles* – concepts and ideas that both of your authors hope and trust you will find helpful and useful not only on the golf course, but also in any and all manner of situations with which life ever seems to confront you.

Under any circumstances we appear to perceive, we now know that we are always free to "choose again"—to think with the part of our mind that understands the truth about what we are, and is not misled by the fear-based thoughts of the fragile, illusory ego.

We no longer see *only the past*, as we now exist "in the zone" and in the eternal moment of *now*. We never forget our function of forgiveness *(or forget our divots, either!)*. We always know that God is right there in our golf bag, and with us at every moment, sustaining us with perfect follow-through in everything we ever do, or ever think of.

And we know that we are always entitled to the metaphysical mulligans known as *Miracles*—the changes in perception and thinking that will lead us out of any difficulty, and into a state of true peace, and endless joy.

May you spend your *Eternity* in this peace...in this *Clubhouse!*

About the Authors

• CHARLOTTE MCGINNIS •

Charlotte McGinnis, a personal development counselor, inter-faith minister, and expert on holistic health and wellness, is the co-founder of *The Art of Living Well Radio Network* on Blog Talk Radio. Charlotte is a success strategist whose passion and purpose is to help people solve problems, define their goals, and create a plan to make it happen.

A leader in the holistic health and spirituality movement, Charlotte founded and shaped *The Palm Beach Center for Living*, which showcased new-thought pioneers including Marianne Williamson, Deepak Chopra, Brian Weiss, Gregg Braden, Neale Donald Walsh, and John Perkins. From its inception in 1994, the Center provided a forum for hundreds of prominent speakers and spiritual seekers and offered outreach programs to disenfranchised men, women and children in Palm Beach County, Florida.

In 1997, Charlotte created the *Zen Golf Center*, marrying her experi-ence in the spiritual arena with her life-long love and achievement in the world of professional golf.

A native of Huntington, West Virginia, Charlotte knew at an early age that she was destined to become a professional golf player. Moving to Florida at age nineteen to pursue her dream, she became a world class player, qualifying for the *U.S. Women's Open* in 1988, and going on to hold professional positions at prestigious golf clubs like *PGA National Golf Club*, *Ibis Country Club*, and *Hunters Run* in Palm Beach County, Florida, and *Quaker Ridge Golf Club* in Westchester, New York.

Charlotte enjoys sharing her insights with others and has lectured in the United States, Canada, the Caribbean, and South America. In the spring of 2009, she became a certified *LifeSuccess Consultant*, which has enabled her to combine spiritual thinking with practical coaching to reach greater audiences with more pertinent and actionable advice. She offers seminars and individual sessions in *Zen Golf*, *A Course in Miracles*, and life and business strategies.

In May 2011, along with three partners, Charlotte opened *Fitness for the Body, Mind and Soul* in Hendersonville, North Carolina, where she is offering *Sunday Soulful Celebration Services*, in addition to *A Course in Miracles* and *Zen Golf* lessons and seminars.

About the Authors

• GENE BOGART •

Gene Bogart comes from an extensive background in broadcasting and entertainment. For many years, he presented *The Gene Bogart Show* on daily drive-time radio for listeners in the Long Island market area, and later served as a director and producer for syndicated radio programming in New York City. He has also written, produced and appeared on-camera for a variety of television and video projects.

Gene is perhaps best known in broadcast and media productions as a professional voiceover artist, having lent his distinctive voice to countless TV and radio commercials, entertainment programs, and metaphysically oriented projects for CD, DVD, and the Internet.

Gene's significant involvement in metaphysical spirituality began in earnest in the early 1990s, when he first met Charlotte McGinnis, and became one of the 'regular volunteer' members at South Florida's *Palm Beach Center For Living*. Since that time, Gene has become one of the best-known voices in the worldwide community of *A Course in Miracles*, due in no small part to his work as creator, producer, and co-host of the highly successful *Gary Renard Podcast* series (available at *iTunes* and at www.**Forgiveness.tv**). The series has routinely been ranked within the *"Top 20"* in the Spirituality category at *iTunes*, often sharing the top ranks with other notables such as Oprah Winfrey and Eckhart Tolle. Gene also portrays the voice of the enlightened teacher *'Arten'* in the audio-book CD recordings of his buddy Gary Renard's bestseller, ***The Disappearance of the Universe***.

195

In 2010, Gene created and continues to host, moderate, and write commentary for an international on-line *Course in Miracles* study and discussion group called ***On Course with Gene Bogart***. He is widely recognized as one of the most popular and effective professional narrators of the complete recorded set of 365 Workbook Lessons of *A Course in Miracles*.

Gene is also a talented musician, singer, songwriter, recording artist, on-stage personality and live-event M.C. In the areas of spirituality and self-development, Gene has worked in the studio with and/or appeared on stage alongside such notables as Marianne Williamson, Deepak Chopra, Doreen Virtue, Gregg Braden, and of course, Gary Renard. This wealth of experience – in addition to hosting and moderating seminar and discussion groups in various areas of the country, on conference calls, and now over the Internet – give Gene a unique perspective in bringing together the concepts of media, entertainment, and enlightenment.

Gene played golf while in college... *rather poorly,* he'll be the first to admit! But he has always maintained a fascinated interest in following the game, and now combines his experiences and perspectives on golf, spirituality, communications, and lighthearted humor into his work as co-author of *A Golf Course in Miracles*.

Gene Bogart lives in South Florida with his lovely wife Helen, and their two sister tuxedo-kittens, Boots and Willie!

Notes & Links

In no particular order, here are some names, information, and contact links for people and organizations we'd like to include here in our book.

http://agcim.com – For general information about *A Golf Course in Miracles* and *The Foundation for Inner Par,* email: *info@agcim.com*

http://acim.org – Website for *The Foundation for Inner Peace:* publisher of the authorized edition(s) of *A Course in Miracles.*

Here are URL listings for our good friends who have endorsed our book:
http://www.garyrenard.com – Gary Renard
http://www.greggbraden.com – Gregg Braden
http://www.asktheo.com – Marcus (and Sheila) Gillette
http://www.garywiren.com – Gary Wiren, Ph.D.
http://www.lifeonpurpose.com – Dr. Brad Swift

AUTHOR: **GENE BOGART**
Personal website: http://www.genebogart.com
(Gene can be emailed at: *gene@agcim.com*)

http://www.forgiveness.tv – *Forgiveness.tv* is the online "home" of the *Gary Renard Podcast* series, which Gene produces and co-hosts. Gene's *Forgiveness/On Course* newsletter list, *"Spoofs"* of the podcasts, links to video clips, and many other features are available at this site as well.
• *"Whatever the question...forgiveness is always the answer!"* •

http://www.oncourse.genebogart.com – The link to the international on-line ACIM study group, *On Course with Gene Bogart.*

197

Author: **CHARLOTTE McGINNIS**
Personal website: **http://www.charlottemcginnis.com**
(Charlotte can be emailed at: *charlotte@agcim.com*)

http://www.consciousconversations.tv – *Conscious Conversations*
offers a presentation of Charlotte's interviews with leaders in the
metaphysical, spiritual, and holistic healing communities.

http://www.fitnessforthebodymindandsoul.com – Charlotte is
one of the partners in this fine organization in Hendersonville, N.C.

http://www.theartoflivingwell.tv – Charlotte co-founded this
BlogTalk Radio network; Char and Gene co-host a weekly AGCIM
program, and there are several other great shows presented there
regularly, with various other hosts (several of whom have web links
listed here, below.)
http://www.lindsaybabich.com
http://www.divinityalliance.org
http://www.doinga360.com
http://www.h2o-kangen.com – (and say 'hello' to Ellen!)

http://www.margaretannlembo.com – Our dear friend Margaret is
also an *Art of Living Well* program host; she owns a legendary South
Florida bookstore and spiritual center, *The Crystal Garden*; and she
has a terrific new book out, titled *Chakra Awakening*.

http://giddyupmikey.com – Our buddy Mikey (Mike Lemieux)
is a true spiritual wild-man...and a really funny dude. In fact, he
has a cool book out, titled, *"Dude, Where's My Jesus-Fish?"* It's
based on the Course, with a lot of great references to Gary Renard's
work – definitely worth checking into. Plus, he helped us out quite
a bit with some publishing-related questions we had about AGCIM.
Giddy-Up, brother Mikey!

http://www.etsy.com/shop/peacebypiececo–Our dear friend Steven
Bath is the creator of the hilarious *spoofs* of our podcasts, in which

198

he created two characters named Boots and Willie – from which our two adorable kitties got their names! He and his wife, Jane (along with their beautiful daughter Gina, and their cool-but-strange son *{and our beloved adopted nephew}* Joey), create some amazing custom mosaic designs. Check out *Peace by Piece* at their website, and also on Facebook.

For information on how we got our wonderful book cover design, and also the professionally rendered version of our *AGCIM* "golf bag logo", please contact **JM Design & Illustration** at *jeanneweb2@ gmail.com*

Back cover photo of the authors taken by **Helen Bogart**.

A big *AGCIM Thank You* for our nifty AGCIM golf-ball and golf-club section and line-break images – as well as for so many uncountable favors in so many ways, for so many years – to Gene's great buddy, **O.J. Dorson**, whom anybody needing a genius tech guy (and hopefully with money to spend) can contact at *oj@thedorsons.com*

http://www.lisatuchekart.com – This is the *new* website for our dear friend Lisa, who has been absolutely the most faithful listener to our *AGCIM radio show* (along with her *possibly* significant-other from the future, *Zontar*.) Lisa, in addition to being a real sweetheart, is a gifted and talented artist, whose beautiful paintings can be viewed at her website, listed here. *(Everyone, please go take a look!)*

And of course, thanks to **Zontar** himself, our stalwart *AGCIM radio program* listener, who hears all of our archived radio programs in the future, where he lives.

We don't have any contact information for him… *Yet!*

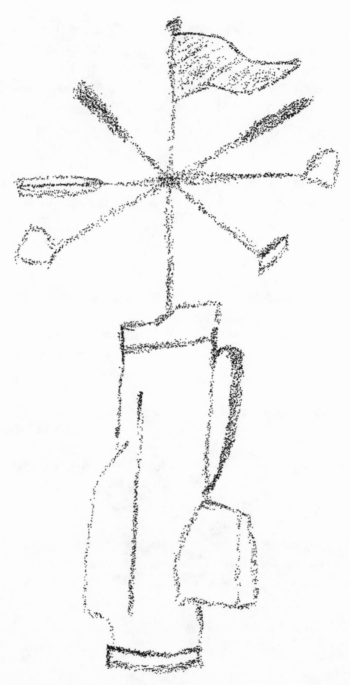

Original "golf bag logo" sketch by Gene Bogart, October 2010

Made in the USA
Charleston, SC
30 May 2012